"Hurry, crowds and noise are enemies of the soul. Our addiction to busyness hides the path to true life. In *The Radical Pursuit of Rest*, John Koessler shows us a more excellent way. It is the way of Christ. Read this book and learn the unforced rhythms of grace."

H. B. Charles Jr., pastor-teacher, Shiloh Metropolitan Baptist Church, Jacksonville, Florida

"Weariness plagues believers today because we have never mastered rest. Demands at work, responsibilities at church and needs at home squeeze rest from our lives leaving us panting and unfulfilled. We desperately need 'the radical pursuit of rest' as expertly explained by Koessler. Drop the chains, pick up this book and learn how to truly refresh your soul with biblical rest."

Paul Nyquist, president, Moody Bible Institute

"When John Koessler writes a book, I read it. His latest volume on the pursuit of rest is a prophetic word to an evangelical subculture that sometimes worships at the altar of productivity. As always, John openly shares his own sometimes-crooked journey towards finding genuine rest and offers some practical help along the way. This excellent book will make you rethink your own goals and how you measure success."

Mark Mitchell, lead pastor, Central Peninsula Church

"We live in a restless world in desperate need of those who would invite us into the restful, unhurried kingdom of God. John Koessler provides just such an invitation. *The Radical Pursuit of Rest* is biblically rich, theologically well-rooted and thoughtful throughout. I encourage you to read it as a good guide into God's gracious and multifaceted gift of rest."

Alan Fadling, executive director, The Leadership Institute, author of *An Unhurried Life*

"Here is the extravagant promise of John Koessler's wise, pastoral book: none of us needs to work harder at rest. Rather, rest is laid at the table of grace, which God himself has prepared. In this way, it is rescue for the weary and hope for the heavy laden. When we realize that God hasn't invited us to share his busyness but enter his rest, we ⸻ ⸻ at's an invitation I can't seem to resist, ⸻ t so clearly and compellingly."

Jen Pollock Michel, author of *Teach U*

D1057327

"Most of us yearn for some R & R, but we set our sights too low. It isn't just that we don't do Sabbaths well. We can hardly imagine what Jesus meant when he said, 'I will give you rest.' John Koessler, with his characteristically lucid and artistic writing, welcomes us into a kind of leisure that does not require us to wait for our day off. *The Radical Pursuit of Rest* helped me see sloth, ambition, technology and even death with biblical eyes."

Lee Eclov, senior pastor, Village Church of Lincolnshire, author of *Pastoral Graces*, contributor to *Preaching Today* and *Leadership Journal*

"Speaking with wisdom and probing insight to a restless, production-driven culture, John Koessler has written a thoughtful, profound and eminently practical book. Like a jeweler, Koessler turns the idea of holy rest slowly in the light, allowing each facet to gleam brightly. It is rare to find a book that is, on the one hand, so deeply theological and, on the other hand, so close to the realities on the ground that it has the potential to change the ways we plan the day."

Thomas G. Long, Bandy Professor of Preaching, Candler School of Theology, Emory University

JOHN KOESSLER

Foreword by **Mark Galli**

THE
RADICAL
PURSUIT
of REST

ESCAPING *the*
PRODUCTIVITY TRAP

IVP Books

An imprint of InterVarsity Press
Downers Grove, Illinois

InterVarsity Press
P.O. Box 1400, Downers Grove, IL 60515-1426
ivpress.com
email@ivpress.com

Published in association with the literary agency of Mark Sweeney & Associates, Bonita Springs, Florida.

InterVarsity Press® is the book-publishing division of InterVarsity Christian Fellowship/USA®, a movement
of students and faculty active on campus at hundreds of universities, colleges and schools of nursing in the
United States of America, and a member movement of the International Fellowship of Evangelical Students.
For information about local and regional activities, visit intervarsity.org.

All Scripture quotations, unless otherwise indicated, are taken from the Holy Bible, New International
Version®. NIV®. Copyright ©1973, 1978, 1984 by International Bible Society. Used by permission of
Zondervan Publishing House. All rights reserved.

While any stories in this book are true, some names and identifying information may have been changed to
protect the privacy of individuals.

Cover design: David Fassett
Interior design: Beth McGill
Images: © TinaFields/iStockphoto

ISBN 978-0-8308-4444-9 (print)
ISBN 978-0-8308-9937-1 (digital)

Printed in the United States of America ∞

Library of Congress Cataloging-in-Publication Data

Koessler, John, 1953-
    The radical pursuit of rest : escaping the productivity trap / John Koessler ; foreword by Mark Galli.
        pages cm
    Includes bibliographical references.
    ISBN 978-0-8308-4444-9 (pbk. : alk. paper)
    1. Rest--Religious aspects--Christianity. I. Title.
    BV4597.55.K64 2016
    248.4'6--dc23

                                                                                2015036059

P 21 20 19 18 17 16 15 14 13 12 11 10 9 8 7 6 5 4 3 2 1

Y 33 32 31 30 29 28 27 26 25 24 23 22 21 20 19 18 17 16

For my sons Drew and Jarred,

with deepest love and an earnest hope

that you will find rest under the easy yoke of Christ.

CONTENTS

FOREWORD

Mark Galli

In the **American Standard Cultural Version** of the Bible we read, "Remember the Sabbath day by keeping it holy, at least in principle. Otherwise, seven days you shall labor and do all your work and shopping, and maybe a couple of times a year take a Sabbath to the LORD your God. Otherwise, make yourself useful, which includes you, your son or daughter, your male or female servant, your animals and any foreigner residing in your towns" (Ex 20:8-10).

Okay, this is not a real version of the Bible, but it is a verse underlined in our hearts and minds. Yes, gentle reader, I point my finger at you—"Behold, the restless one!" But of course, three fingers are pointing back at me.

Some people argue, rightly, that we live in a sex-saturated culture, and that this makes obedience in sexual matters a mighty challenge today. But it is more true that we live in a culture saturated with activity and anxiety, and that this makes obedience to the fourth commandment nearly impossible—harder than living in sexual righteousness. When it comes to commandments six (adultery) and ten (coveting, lusting), we're vigilant. Adultery is scorned and disciplined, and lust (think pornography especially) is shameful. But we hardly bat an eye when someone uses Sunday as they would any other day of the week.

This is not a call for a renewal of Sabbatarian laws. Our attitude toward the Sabbath, however, is a huge neon sign that advertises how deeply committed we are to the commandments of advanced consumer capitalism: seven days you shall labor and shop, and in between cart children to sports leagues, teach Sunday school, volunteer at the homeless shelter, mow the lawn and fall asleep exhausted watching the evening news. We have no doubt that God has the words to eternal life—life that not only lasts and lasts, but overflows with abundance and peace. And yet we have the hardest time living as if this were true.

On top of that—and here's the interesting conundrum—few of us are happy living this way! I know I'm not. The mantras "I'm so busy" and "I have no time" and "I'm so tired" have become for us like a liturgical prayer, ending implicitly with "Lord, have mercy!"

What's going on here?

A lot. The state we find ourselves in has evolved slowly in our culture. It's complicated. I'm guessing that every reader of this book does not waste much time. I'm guessing that everything you do helps others or promotes kingdom work or glorifies God in some way. And when someone gets on a "Remember the Sabbath" jag, you're thinking, All well and good, but what good thing am I to give up exactly?

Then again, the all-powerful and never tiring Creator of the universe thought rest a pretty good idea: "For in six days the LORD made the heavens and the earth, the sea, and all that is in them, but he rested on the seventh day" (Ex 20:11). God resting, of course, is an anthropomorphism: describing God as if he were a human being. In fact, God is always at work, sustaining the universe, nanosecond by nanosecond. If he ever stopped doing that, the universe would disappear into the deepest of black holes. That's one reason some theologians describe God as "pure act." Anything less would signal our end.

And yet they can also describe God as "pure rest"—a being so complete and perfect there is nothing more to be done or said to complete that perfection, only a glorious existence to behold and enjoy. I believe we can read the Genesis text in this way as well. God creates six days and rests on the Sabbath, the text explains. And the theologian surmises: God is both pure act and pure rest.

In fact, it is precisely because God is pure act—never ceasing to uphold the universe by the power of his Word—that we can take a Sabbath and really rest, knowing that God still has the whole universe in his hands. And because God is pure rest, we know he is the perfect reality we are called to behold and enjoy. God's call for us to rest is not just about recharging our batteries for another week of work. It's mostly a command to set apart time and space many times a week to realize and live into the amazing reality that is to come—and is in part already ours in Christ: eternal life. Forever, yes. And for now.

This book is about much more than the literal Sabbath. It includes some wise words about that day, to be sure. But it also includes insights and practices that can help us live a Sabbath life, nanosecond by nanosecond, while we fulfill God's very active call day to day. To radically pursue rest does not mean to take up a new bag of tricks and perform a new list of duties. Yes, there are spiritual practices that can help. But the practices are paradoxical: they are things we do (take the spiritual discipline of silence) that teach us how to stop doing!

As a man addicted to activity and anxiety, I could tell you story after story about how a restless lifestyle is everything from silly to stupid to soul killing. I think you get that. Instead, you need to hear from John Koessler, who has more than a few insights about the culture of restlessness and some wise guidance about building a life in the perfect One we are destined to behold and joy forever.

INTRODUCTION

After I graduated from high school I got a job in a factory that made automobile parts. There were skilled craftsmen who worked at this factory, but I was not one of them. I was an unskilled laborer whose work consisted mostly of pushing buttons on pounding machines that smelled of oil and steel. Every hour a whistle sounded, requiring us to take a five-minute break. This was a safety measure, intended to keep us from being careless with the great machines. There was an obligatory lunch break secured for us by the union. There were also many moments of waiting for others farther up the line to perform their tasks.

The work I did was not hard but it was monotonous. Often the assembly line I was on had a quota for the number of parts it was expected to produce. When the counter reached that number we were done for the day. We were not allowed to make any more parts, but weren't permitted to leave the factory either. So we whiled away the remainder of our time sitting in the cafeteria waiting for our shift to end.

I usually had no notion of what the parts I made actually did or where they fit into the finished vehicle. To me they were metal shapes adorned with clips. I suppose it could be said that I did not really *make* anything. I pushed the button that told the machine to perform its task and then watched the part move down the line or else lifted the part from the machine and carried it to a waiting bin. Indeed, this work was so easy that it was difficult for me to call it work at all. As a result, my time there was marked by tedium more than anything else. The boredom of the work itself was complemented by the greater boredom of the rest that followed it. Neither was especially satisfying.

Rest and work go together. "The sleep of a laborer is sweet, whether he eats little or much," the author of Ecclesiastes observes, "but the abundance of a rich man permits him no sleep" (Eccles 5:12). In our common experience it is work that gives meaning to our rest and rest that provides energy for our work. In this equation work is at the center. Remove work and rest becomes meaningless, perhaps even impossible. Rest in this paradigm exists for the sake of work.

But work, while meaningful, is not meaningful in itself. The writer of Ecclesiastes praises the sleep of the laborer but laments the futility of work. "What does man gain from all his labor at which he toils under the sun?" (Eccles 1:3). This is the first question raised in his book. It is also its primary complaint. While work is meaningful and God uses our work to provide for us, work alone cannot give meaning to our lives. Theologian Josef Pieper observes, "To serve some other purpose is the essential characteristic of work."[1] Work is the servant, not the master. However, we live in an age in which work has become an end in itself.

In our world the craftsman has been displaced by the worker. While the craftsman's work has a telos, or purpose, the worker merely engages in a task. Both make an effort. But the craftsman has the end in view and can see the finished result. The worker usually does not. In such an environment work devolves into a series of tasks performed for a prescribed period of time. Because of this the task never ends. It is only interrupted. When the hand on the clock reaches the appointed hour, we cease. When the hour to start comes around, we begin again. Our work becomes endless and eventually pointless.

When work loses its purpose and becomes an end in itself, rest also loses its meaning. This is not because rest serves work. Neither is it because work justifies rest. It is because rest in its rightful place needs nothing to justify it. Rest is an end in itself. We do not work in order to justify the fact that we rest. We do not rest in order to work. Rest as the Bible describes it is our destiny. It is what we were made for. In this book I am arguing for the radical pursuit of rest.

I should confess at the outset that I am not a radical. I do not live in a cave like St. Anthony or espouse an ascetic lifestyle. I reside in a suburban neighborhood in Northwest Indiana. I take the train to work every morning. I like to watch television at night with my wife by my side and my dog on my lap. I say this because I am afraid the title of this book might give readers the wrong impression. When I write about the radical pursuit of rest, I am not speaking of a life that can be lived by only a select few. Christ's invitation in Matthew 11:29 is addressed to all who labor and are heavy laden. But in a world made up of workers, rest itself is a radical notion. In a church that believes that worshipers must also be workers in order to justify their presence, rest is an uncommon experience. I am not arguing that we pursue rest by radical means. Rather, it is the pursuit of rest itself that is radical.

I should also confess that at one point or another during the writing of this book I have violated every principle I describe in it. I do not and cannot counsel perfection. I write for ordinary people who hope to experience the easy yoke of Christ in the midst of struggle under normal circumstances—not the spiritual elite. You do not have to be a radical to engage in the radical pursuit of rest. You do not have to be perfect before you can experience it. Rest is not reserved for the monk, the priest, the nun or the pastor. It is God's gift offered to common people who work at ordinary jobs.

Still, the idea of pursuing rest may seem like a contradiction in terms. Doesn't working at rest mean the end result is not rest at all? The Bible describes rest as both a destination and a gift. Jesus invites us to receive rest from him as a gift of grace. At the same time we are urged to "make every effort" to enter that rest (Heb 4:11). Rest comes to us, but we can also fall short of rest.

I will make practical suggestions along the way. Some will be very concrete. But this is not really a "how-to" book. The secret to rest is not in what we do so much as in how we see. Rest is both a location and an identity. It is a realm in which we exist. Rest is synonymous with grace, which is never seized by force but always taken hold of freely by faith. Rest is also synonymous with Christ, who is both its primary proponent and chief architect. The first step in the radical pursuit of rest is to seek Christ. This is also the last step. When you find Christ, you will find rest.

RESTLESS FAITH

I do not go to sleep easily. When I do sleep, I sleep lightly. I often wake in the middle of the night, disturbed by the creaking of the house as it shifts on its foundation or startled by the rustle of the dog as she turns in her bed. My wife's breathing beside me is quiet, rhythmic as an incoming tide. But in the distance I hear the shriek of an ambulance and I wonder whose misfortune it laments. I replay the events of the day in my mind, reviewing its conversations and improving my contribution with imagined repartee. I brood over the past. I fret about the future. As the clock on the nightstand counts down the remaining hours, I lie in the dark and wait for the window to brighten with the gray light of dawn.

Apparently I am not the only one who is awake. According to the National Sleep Foundation, more than half of all Americans say they have problems sleeping at night.[1] We are a sleep-deprived culture.

The church suffers from a similar problem. Not from sleep deprivation so much as from a deficit of rest. Today's congregation is a frenetic place. Our worship is marked by frenzied devotion that has full congregational participation as its primary goal. The drummer marks the tempo for the first song and we stand to sing. We remain standing through the entire song service. We are urged to lift our hands or clap in an approach to worship that sees it as a full-body experience. Between songs the worship leader tells us to fan out and find someone to whom we can introduce ourselves. The pastor reminds us to stop by the information desk and sign up for the latest congregational project and then spend time chatting over coffee with someone in the vestibule.

There is considerable enthusiasm in all of this but not much quietness or contemplation. Indeed, in such an atmosphere quietness and contemplation would be frowned on. Contemplation is liable to be interpreted as disengagement or, even worse, dead orthodoxy. Quietness is seen more as awkward silence than a mark of spiritual reflection.

In other churches the start of worship is signaled by the reedy call of the organ. Although there are no drums here, there is just as much activity. But in this case the pressure is focused on worship attendance and involvement in church programs. Those who love Jesus should be present whenever the church doors are open. To be about Christ's business means to attend to the church's business. This church's members are expected to serve on committees, teach Sunday school and listen to children say verses on Wednesday night. At least some (about twenty percent) do. The rest feel ill at ease, trying not to look the pastor in the eye as he or she issues the latest appeal for more help in the nursery.

Both kinds of churches reflect an underlying assumption about our relationship with God and the nature of the Christian life. It is the assumption that busier is better. This assumption in turn is based on the supposition that devotion equals activity. The more we love Christ, the more we will do for him. Those who love Christ the most, whether churches or individuals, will do the most. Since our devotion to Christ should know no bounds, neither should our activity. No matter what we are doing now, we should do more. No matter what we have done in the past, it has not been enough.

THE CULTURE OF PRODUCTIVITY

The result is a highly driven church that constantly strives to exceed its current level of activity. If attendance has grown, it should increase further. If programs have expanded, they must expand even more. Every year the church rolls out new initiatives the way automobile companies roll out new models. Like the latest-model car, the latest project needs to be more impressive than the last. The church is driven by the bottom line just as much as a company whose lifeblood is sales revenue. Only in the church's case the bottom line is measured primarily in people and what they do. It is only secondarily viewed in dollars and cents. However, the two are related. If you have more people, you have more resources. The most "successful" church has plenty of both.

These assumptions have had a profound effect on the church's culture of leadership. Today's church leaders have been shaped by the corporate world where productivity is the summum bonum of the organization. Business writers like Jim Collins, Patrick Lencioni and Seth Godin have as much to say about how the church operates as the Bible does. It might be said that they influence the church's culture of leadership even more than the Bible, since the Scriptures do not speak with the degree of specificity that we would like on the pragmatic matters that are of greatest importance to us.

The Bible does not describe how to have a successful church—at least not as we define success today. As a result, where leadership and ministry strategy are concerned, we are more interested in results than in theological reflection. We adopt the latest ministry methods without critical appraisal. The only test we employ is to ask what the method has done for others and whether it will work for us. What's more, our methods often work. But methodologies also impart ethos. Neil Postman's observation about tools also holds true for methods. Postman warns that there is an ideological bias embedded in every tool, "a predisposition to construct the world as one thing rather than another, to value one thing over another, to amplify one sense or skill or attitude more loudly than another."[2]

> The community of believers is no longer a kingdom of priests but a service industry whose primary mission is to provide spiritual goods and services to the masses.

The ethos of the marketplace is one that combines utilitarianism with consumerism. In the marketed culture of the church, God is treated like a product. One might even say that he is less than a product since the marketed church is not really selling God or even the gospel. It is selling itself. The contemporary church is seeking to create an atmosphere that will attract worshipers and persuade them to return. The community of believers is no longer a kingdom of priests but a service industry whose primary mission is to provide spiritual goods and services to the masses. Visitors are treated like consumers and the church's members are employees whose main job is to promote the brand. They do not worship; they produce. We call the things we do to get results "being effective." But we call the results "God's blessing."

BUSY PREACHING

The church's preaching is equally busy, chock-full of moral imperatives, practical advice and five-step methods. Every sermon poses a new challenge that can be resolved by applying the right combination of faith and effort. The problems vary but the solution is the same. Christ is the answer, of course. He always is. He is all-powerful. But apparently his unlimited power is of little help unless we learn how to apply the right mix of Scripture, faith, prayer and sanctified elbow grease. God is waiting for us to act. We sometimes feel when listening to these sermons that although we are saved by grace, it's really the effort that counts.

Each week the pastor urges the congregation toward greater exertion. Congregants are told that they must round the bases from mere attendance to full involvement. They are Christ's hands and feet. Church attendance is good, but it is not enough. Fully devoted followers of Jesus join a small group and engage in service projects. They serve in the nursery and come out on weekends to rake leaves for the elderly. They spend their vacation doing short-term ministry. They run for office or become political activists. They join the school board and support the arts. It goes without saying that in all of this real Christians keep the family a top priority. And the time they spend in God's Word should be measured in hours rather than minutes.

These are the shadowlands of grace, where the line is blurred between what God alone can do for us and what we must do for ourselves. We may not be legalists in the technical sense, but we do inhabit a region that shares a border with legalism. As writer and *Christianity Today* editor Mark Galli has observed, "What I'm hearing time and again, in every corner of the church I visit, is not the soaring message of grace but the dull message of works—that I have to believe a certain theological construct, or have a certain feeling, or perspire in effort before I can be assured of God's radical acceptance and my future salvation."[3]

What the church needs is rest. But it is a special kind of rest. We need the rest that only Christ can provide. The rest of Christ is both a remedy and a relief. But more than anything else it is a gift. Jesus describes its character in Matthew 11:28-30: "Come to me, all you who are weary and burdened, and I will give you rest. Take my yoke upon you and learn from me, for I am gentle and humble in heart, and you will find rest for your souls. For my yoke is easy and my burden is light."

We should not take lightly the fact that Jesus addresses this invitation to all who are "weary" and "burdened." Jesus was a laborer. He was a carpenter and the son of a carpenter (Mt 13:55; Mk 6:3). He knew the weight of a load and shared the experience of all who ply a trade. Jesus was familiar with the roughhewn contour of unshaped wood and the pleasing weight of the proper tool. He felt the weariness that comes at dusk when strength ebbs along with the light. Jesus was also a wanderer who knew the rigors of travel. It was Jesus who sat down by Jacob's well, "tired as he was from the journey" (Jn 4:6). Yet the weariness he speaks of in his invitation does not come from ordinary exertion. Common labor may tire the body but there is also a weariness that afflicts the soul.

WEARINESS OF THE SOUL

In 1901 a scientist named Duncan McDougall believed he could ascertain the weight of the soul. He tried to accomplish this by measuring the weight of six patients as they died. Based on his experiments, he concluded that the human soul weighed twenty-one grams. Unfortunately subsequent attempts to reproduce McDougall's experiments were unsuccessful, leading scientists to conclude that his methods were flawed and the results invalid.

Yet even if the soul is weightless, it is clear that it can be weighed down. Our personal experience is proof enough that such burdens are real, even if they cannot be calculated in grams or pounds.

The soul can be burdened by anxiety (Prov 12:25), a state of mind in which concern is amplified by fear. The concern itself is often legitimate, which is the very thing that enables fear to grow so easily. When Jesus warned his disciples not to worry about what they would eat, drink or wear in Matthew 6:25, he was not implying that such concerns were trivial. If we don't eat, we die. Food is necessary to life. Clothing is necessary too, required by most cultures for both warmth and modesty. Even God recognizes this—food and clothing were among the first things he provided for those he created. When God placed Adam in the Garden of Eden, he gave him the freedom to eat of all the trees but one (Gen 2:15-17). After Adam and Eve sinned, God replaced the makeshift garments they had thrown together with garments of skin he crafted especially for them (Gen 3:21).

Jesus acknowledges that food and clothing are necessities in Matthew 6:32. And it is this very recognition that underlies his instruction to cast worry aside. Why shouldn't we be anxious about such things? Because God already knows we need them. He always has. Anxiety as Jesus diagnoses it is not the result of misdirected concern so much as it is a consequence of misaligned confidence. We feel the weight of anxiety because we have placed our trust in the wrong thing. We depend on the means of production. Or we rely on the things that are produced. Jesus says all these things come from the hand of God. As he puts it, there is more to life (literally, the soul) than food and more to the body than clothing (Mt 6:25).

Jesus indicates that we have more important things to worry about. There is a life that is greater than physical life and a death that is worse than physical death. We have better things to pursue than food and clothing. It is the pagan who runs after these things; this is what people do when they have no God.

But more than anything else, Jesus' words direct our attention beyond our daily concerns to one who is greater than they are. He redirects our focus from the concerns themselves to the one who is concerned for us. We do not need to be anxious about food and clothing because our heavenly Father knows we need them. Thus the weight of anxiety is the soul's misapprehension. It is the thinking of people who see themselves as orphaned. Such anxiety is the anguished cry of a soul that has forgotten it has a Father in heaven.

ALL WHO LABOR

The overburdened soul does not always manifest itself in depression. It can also go to the opposite extreme. In Luke 21:34 Jesus warns, "Be careful, or your hearts will be weighed down with dissipation, drunkenness and the anxieties of life, and that day will close on you unexpectedly like a trap." The Greek word translated as "dissipation" referred in Jesus' day to the giddiness that comes with drinking too much wine. It is interesting that dissipation and drunkenness are linked here with the anxieties of life. In this case it would seem that the heart is not depressed but overstimulated. The agitation that comes with anxiety can be just as paralyzing as depression and often leads to it.

It is often tempting to resort to artificial means in an effort to cope. The drug of choice mentioned in Luke 21:34 is alcohol. But not all artificial means of coping are chemical. Many of us rely on our careers to define who we are as persons, to order our world and to satisfy our desires. In its ordinary and healthy form, work serves as a means to an end. But in its narcotic and distorted form, work turns into a distraction and eventually becomes an end in itself. The nature of the task may not change at all. The work we do may be virtuous and even necessary. It is our relationship to work that has become destructive.

This distortion of work sometimes manifests itself in the addictive behavior known as "workaholism." But it also reflects an approach to life itself. The resulting inversion creates a world where work exists for work's own sake. It is what Josef Pieper calls "the world of total work."[4] He observes that this kind of world is always poor and impoverished, even when its inhabitants are rich in material goods. This is because everything and everyone in it is subjected to the rationalist and utilitarian principles that shape its values. Work is more than a distraction. It is more than an addiction. Work has become a religion.[5] In a world where a person's worth is measured by usefulness, all things are subordinated to work.

In such an inverted world, it is not enough for worshipers to contemplate the beauty of Christ. Those who gather for worship must justify their presence by doing something useful. Believers who come to church intent only on worship are treated like spiritual slackers. Meanwhile congregational worship itself is described from the pulpit in terms that suggest that it is the lowest and least valued form of spiritual devotion. Many pastors and worship leaders urge church attenders to get more involved by suggesting that the worship service is only the "first base" of devotion. This gives the impression that the worship service is primarily for visitors and beginners. The truly committed will volunteer for the nursery or join a small group.

There are certainly motives that can defile our worship. Jesus denounced the prayers of those who were more intent on being seen by others than being heard by God (Mt 6:5), and he spoke scornfully of the kind of blathering prayer offered by those who "think they will be heard for their many words" (Mt 6:7). These two approaches to prayer have different audiences. One is a display intended to impress fellow worshipers. The other is addressed to God. Yet both place the emphasis on performance. In the former it is not enough to speak to God; one must be *seen* speaking to God. In the latter it is not enough to speak simply; we must bowl God over with our words to gain his ear.

But ministry too can be defiled. It is possible to be engaged in ministry and be self-absorbed at the same time. Paul's observation that in Corinth everyone had a hymn, a word of instruction, a revelation, a tongue or an interpretation was a description of the church's ministry style but it was also an implied criticism (1 Cor 14:26). His assertion that such things "must be done for the strengthening of the church" was as cautionary as it was explanatory. Paul did not find fault with the church's participatory style but with the self-centered manner in which it was executed. Corinthian worship and ministry were so mixed with egoism that their meetings did more harm than good (1 Cor 11:17). Activity alone, even when it is spiritually directed, is not identical with virtue.

FINDING YOUR COMFORT ZONE

When work is no longer a means but becomes an end itself, we end up valuing strenuous effort above all else. As a result, we see difficulty as more than a necessary component of completing a meaningful task—difficulty becomes its own virtue. This too has spiritual consequences. When effort itself becomes a virtue, we no longer take up the cross in order to identify with Christ or even to mortify the flesh but we carry the cross for its own sake. We sweat and suffer because we think of these things themselves as merits. It was this kind of thinking that poisoned the ascetic ideal of the early church and sometimes turned the monk's cell into a torture chamber.

Admittedly, we are not as rigorous as the desert fathers. Most of us do not take to the caves and attempt to perfect our souls through deprivation and physical suffering. But many of us share their ethos. In fact, we hear an echo of this ethos in the dictum that God wants us to "get out of our comfort zone." Being comfortable, it would seem, is a bad thing. As long as we are comfortable, we cannot pursue God's will. Only by making ourselves uncomfortable can we please God.

In this way of thinking, discomfort becomes more than an occasional side effect of obedience or an environment in which we are sometimes asked to exercise faith. It is now a destination. Discomfort is a mark of grace. It is proof of our genuine devotion. Steeped as we are in such a culture, we might be startled to discover that a theologian as eminent and ancient as Thomas Aquinas asserted the opposite. Aquinas observed,

"The essence of virtue consists in the good rather than the difficult."[6] He noted that not everything that is difficult is necessarily more meritorious.

Such thinking is hard for us to accept. Josef Pieper explains why: "The inmost significance of the exaggerated value which is set upon hard work appears to be this: man seems to mistrust everything that is effortless; he can only enjoy, with a good conscience, what he has acquired with toil and trouble; he refuses to have anything as a gift."[7]

It is even more disorienting to hear Christ's invitation in Matthew 11:28-30. Amazingly, Jesus does not call us to leave our comfort zone but to find it. He invites us to cast weariness and labor aside and to seek the comfort of his rest. If the invitation seems odd to those who know nothing other their own haggard effort, the proffered remedy sounds stranger still. Jesus does not advise us to organize our lives more responsibly and create some space for rest. Jesus speaks of rest as something we "find." This kind of language reveals an important dimension to this rest. It is objective in the sense that it lies outside of ourselves. Rest is not an inner state that can be produced by thinking a certain way or placing ourselves in the right conditions. It is obtained only by entering into a relationship. When we find Christ, we find rest.

Jesus' language also implies something about us. He seems to indicate that rest is what we have been looking for all along. There is a double entendre in these words. We have been laboring—but for what? Jesus does not say. Whatever its goal, it is clear that our labor has earned us nothing. We have come up empty.

With this invitation Jesus turns both rest and work on their heads. The rest we once sought turns out to be arduous labor. But in the reoriented world of the kingdom, we are given a new vocation and a new identity. In the inverted world of total work, we were less than slaves—we were cogs in a great machinery of effort. But now that we have received the yoke of Christ we find a rest we could not have achieved by our own effort. Although the yoke indicates that we are still servants, Jesus' promise reveals that we are more than his slaves. This is the promise of a friend (Jn 15:15).

It is tempting to approach the problem of restlessness as merely a lack of discipline. If this were the case, the solution would require just a little more structure on our part. But this is a little like treating alcoholism with whiskey. It leads us to think the problem can be solved by adopting the proper technique or applying the right kind of pressure. We might try to be less driven. We could acquire skills that enable us to manage our daily schedule. We might discipline ourselves to take a day off now and then. Or perhaps we could find someone to help us organize our lives, the way some people hire a consultant to help them remove the clutter from their closets. Maybe all we need to do is to be more regular in our observance of the Sabbath.

None of these things is necessarily bad. Indeed, they might do us some practical good. But they are not the solution. We are suffering from a malady with roots that go deeper than our schedule. Certainly we are busy. We may even be too busy. But busyness is not the heart of our problem. We are suffering from a condition far worse than burnout. It is not a vacation that we need but something else that only Jesus can provide. What we need is a yoke.

THE YOKE OF REST

Jesus the carpenter would have been well familiar with the yoke as an implement of agriculture. A piece of wood shaped to fit over the neck of animals that have been drafted to pull a heavy load, the yoke seems a most unlikely metaphor to use in conjunction with the idea of rest. What could be more antithetical than to be compared to a beast of burden? As a farm implement the yoke was itself a burden and its function was to enable the animal who wore it to bear someone else's load. No wonder the yoke is a common symbol of submission and oppression in Scripture (Gen 27:40; Ex 6:6-7; 1 Kings 12:4; Is 9:4; 10:27; Gal 5:1; 1 Tim 6:1).

The yoke, after all, was more than a tool. It was an instrument of exploitation. The yoke was the means the farmer used to gain full advantage of the animal's strength. It is true that the beast received a kind of benefit from the yoke. It enabled him to bear the weight of the load. But the load itself was a burden the animal would never have taken up if not for the intrusion of the farmer. The farmer thinks nothing of it. To the farmer the only reason the animal exists is to bear such burdens. The animal thinks nothing of it either, since it is a brute beast and lacks the capacity to reason. But we are not animals. We do not want to be anyone's beast of burden. Why would Jesus think such an image would appeal to us?

The answer is that we are already under a yoke. Wendell Berry is right: "We are all to some extent the products of an exploitive society, and it would be foolish and self-defeating to pretend that we do not bear its stamp."[8] It would be equally foolish to pretend that the church does not bear its stamp. When Berry contrasts the values of the exploiter with those of the nurturer, it is hard not to feel that the contemporary church lines up on the wrong side: "The exploiter is a specialist, an expert; the nurturer is not. The standard of the exploiter is efficiency; the standard of the nurturer is care."[9] The exploiter's primary interest is return on investment. The nurturer is concerned about health. As a result, Berry explains, "The exploiter thinks in terms of numbers, quantities, 'hard facts'; the nurturer in terms of character, condition, quality, kind."[10]

Of course, we do not consider what we do in the church exploitation. We have more spiritual words to describe our values and behavior. We speak of our programs and our efforts at branding as positioning and contextualization rather than consumerism. Our congregational busyness is a way to activate the ministry of our members, not use them. We justify our actions by saying that we are only trying to be effective. Perhaps we are.

Yet despite our obsessive quest for effectiveness, our best efforts do not seem to produce the quality of life that Jesus describes in his invitation. The yokes we have built for ourselves do not seem easy. They chafe. Nor do the burdens we have taken upon ourselves (and those we try to lay on others) feel light. They are as wearisome as any ordinary work, more like the drudgery of the assembly line than the glorious incursion of a kingdom.

Meanwhile God in his dealings with the church betrays a disturbing lack of interest in effectiveness as we have defined it. He does not seem interested in numbers. The people he sends to us are not strategic at all. They are a rabble who look more like the laborers, hookers and marginal people that Jesus consorted with in the Gospels than the gifted individuals we had hoped would fill out our ranks. And they are far from

> The people God sends to us are not strategic at all. They are a rabble who look more like the laborers, hookers and marginal people that Jesus consorted with in the Gospels than the gifted individuals we had hoped would fill out our ranks.

effective. Their lives, if they are not a complete shambles, are at least in serious disarray. No wonder we prefer our elegant systems to the roughhewn implement Jesus offers. But our systems have failed us, as have our aspirations and our desires. Even the cloying scent of our own success has left us sick.

The yoke of rest that Jesus offers can be taken, but it cannot be seized by force. We do not manage ourselves into it, acquire it by bargain or even attain it by discipline. Rest as Jesus describes it must be done for us. On the surface it might sound like rest exists apart from Christ—as though Jesus could give us rest the way a parent gives a coin to a small child. But Jesus is the subject of the verb in Matthew 11:28 and we are the object. What Jesus says might be translated something like "I will rest you" or "I will refresh you." This rest is as relational as it is experiential. We come to Christ and he refreshes us. We do not come to Christ, receive our rest and then go our way. By offering us rest, Christ offers himself.

During the long nights when I lie awake in bed, I cannot will myself to sleep. I clear my mind of the day's events and imagine myself lying on the beach. I attempt to match my breathing to the quiet rhythm of my wife's. I count down from one hundred. I pray. But nothing works. The more I pursue it, the more elusive sleep is. Yet if I wait long enough, sleep will eventually claim me. Despite my longing and the long delay, slumber's arrival always seems sudden. Sleep comes to me as a surprise, greeting me like a lover who embraces me from behind. So it is with the rest of Christ. When we find Christ, we are surprised to find rest. We are surprised to discover that rest is what we have been seeking all along: "Thou awakest us to delight in Thy praise; for Thou madest us for Thyself, and our heart is restless, until it rest in Thee."[11]

QUESTIONS FOR REFLECTION

1. Should church make us feel rested or energized? Is it possible for worship to be too "busy"? Why or why not? Why do you think quietness is so rare in our worship culture?

2. What does a successful church look like? If success is not measured in numbers or resources, how should we measure it? How might it affect the church if it ignored the question of success altogether?

3. How do people use busyness as a form of self-medication? Why do you think they do this?

4. Theologian Thomas Aquinas observed, "The essence of virtue consists in the good rather than the difficult." What is the difference?

5. When does the church's desire to motivate and mobilize its members become exploitation? What can it do to guard against this?

THE GOD
WHO RESTS

When my eldest son, Drew, was a toddler, bedtime was a battleground in our house. I think he felt cheated by the prospect of sleep. He hated the thought of going to bed while the rest of the world continued on. Instead of welcoming rest, Drew confronted it. He steeled himself against the prospect of sleep the way a wrestler braces himself to meet an opponent. "No night-night! No night-night!" he cried in indignation.

To no avail. He was consigned to his crib by the superior force of parental authority. One night my wife walked past his door and heard him muttering to himself. There was nothing left for him to do but mutter. "Stay awake! Stay awake!" he commanded himself.

The prospect of sleep can be unnerving. While we sleep the world continues to be active. We are oblivious to our surroundings, supine and powerless. We are not in control during sleep but must depend on the mercy and protection of God. Our vulnerability is captured in the familiar children's prayer:

Now I lay me down to sleep,
I pray the Lord my soul to keep.
If I should die before I wake,
I pray the Lord my soul to take.

This was the first prayer I ever prayed. I am sure it was intended to teach me about God's care, but I learned something else. Though designed to bring me comfort, this prayer served as a nightly reminder of my vulnerability and mortality. It implied that while I slept my soul was in danger and that I needed protection (it did not say from what). It told me I might die during the night. What's more, if such a terrible fate did overtake me, God would "take" my soul. The prayer did not say what he would do with it. There was something unfriendly in this language, especially when used in conjunction with the word "keep." This sounded uncomfortably like theft to me. I did not want to die in my sleep. I did not want God to take my soul. I wanted to keep it and wake up the next morning. No wonder I was reluctant to close my eyes.

Like sleep, rest too can be unnerving. For those who value activism, rest seems unproductive. We cannot work while we rest. Rest is delay. It squanders precious time and diverts us from our goal. Rest erodes our competitive edge. Devoting ourselves to rest does not seem like a good strategy for getting ahead. When we rest, we drop out of the race and yield the advantage to others. After all, it was while the hare napped that the tortoise won the race. The world in which we live and work values perfect attendance and admires those who are always busy. No employer has ever given an award to someone because they took a regular vacation.

When it comes to ministry, our values are much the same. We

admire those who burn brightly and flame out more than we do those measured souls who shine with an even light. We calculate the miles John Wesley traveled during his forty years of itinerate ministry or the number of hours he preached. We look up to those pastors of old who were so devoted to ministry that they ruined their health and died at a young age. We suspect that the measure of our ministry success is inversely proportional to the amount of space that remains in our appointment book. The smaller the margin we have left for leisure, the more successful we must be.

In such an environment rest is an emergency measure rather than a primary pursuit. We rest out of necessity. We may step out of the race for a time but we do so reluctantly and only so that we can reenter it with renewed vigor. We see the value of rest but not for its own sake. We feel that we must first justify rest before we can indulge in it.

THE GOD WHO RESTS

In a YOLO world that believes it's better to burn out than rust out, it seems strange to consider that God was the first to rest. According to Genesis 2:2, "By the seventh day God had finished the work he had been doing; so on the seventh day he rested from all his work." This sounds like a page torn from ancient myth—especially when we note the context. The seventh day is the climax of God's week of creation. He labors for six days and rests on the seventh. Is it because he is exhausted from all his labors? This is surely how the old gods would have been portrayed.

But this first portrait of God found in the Bible distinguishes the Creator from his creation. Creation depends on God for its origin but God depends on no one. This sets the Bible's creation narrative apart among the world's religions. The Creator is not served by human hands and does not need anything. He gives life and breath to everyone.

In view of God's power and supremacy over creation, we should not understand the rest spoken of in Genesis as restorative for God. We humans need rest, but God is not like us. When we work we grow weary. God never becomes weary. Yet neither was the rest of God merely symbolic. When the biblical text asserts that God rested, it means what it says. Despite the mythic tone of the assertion, it happened. On the seventh day God rested from all his work. Similarly, God's rest was more than an example. God did not merely appear to rest in order to make a point, the way a parent might pretend to sleep to encourage an unwilling child to take a nap. God's rest is a pattern for us, but there was more than modeling going on here. God's rest is the rest of completion rather than restoration. On the seventh day all God's work was finished.

> God's rest is the rest of completion rather than restoration.

This was the way Jesus understood the rest of God as well. When the religious leaders condemned him for healing on the Sabbath, he appealed to God's rest in his defense. According to John 5:17, "Jesus said to them, 'My Father is always at his work to this very day, and I, too, am working.'" This is more than a simple assertion that the Father worked through Jesus to heal the invalid at the pool of Bethesda on that particular Sabbath day. Jesus' words allude to the rest spoken of in Genesis 2:2, implying that the Creator enjoys a perpetual Sabbath. God is always at work in his creation, but he is also always at rest.[1]

This is difficult (perhaps impossible) for us to fully grasp. It sounds like a contradiction because we are timebound and can experience God's work only as a sequence of linear events. For us purpose and action are always distinct from one another. We purpose and then we do. More accurately, we purpose and then we attempt to do. But God is not like this. His purpose is more than aspiration. For God to will is to do. His relationship to time is also radically different from ours. God acts in time but does not relate to time the same way we do. For God "a day is like a thousand years, and a thousand years are like a day" (2 Pet 3:8). We get a glimpse of the difference in those passages that seem to conflate the past, present and future. For example, Jesus is described as the "Lamb that was slain from the creation of the world" (Rev 13:8). The kingdom will be given to those for whom it has been prepared "since the creation of world" (Mt 25:34).

The work God does in the present brings that which God has purposed in eternity past into the realm of our experience. As far as God's purpose is concerned this work is already finished. Viewed from the perspective of our experience it is new or yet to be accomplished. This fact makes God's rest in Genesis the fountainhead of all rest. It also makes God's rest the starting point for all Christian practice. The things we do for God are an extension of his workmanship and proceed from God's finished work. The good works we do are those "God prepared in advance for us to do" (Eph 2:10). Work and rest both begin with God.

My father was an artist. He had a black leather sketchbook filled with cartoons and doodles. As a boy I was enthralled by his drawings and wondered how I could learn to draw like him. I began by tracing over his originals line for line. Once I got a feel for the shape of the image, I drew my own copy next to his. At first my images looked like the childish imitations they were.

But in time it was hard to tell which drawings were mine and which were my father's. We often view the Christian life this way. It is the imitation of Christ. But when we live the Christian life, we are not merely tracing over the lines of Christ's example in an attempt to reproduce the contours of his life in our experience. It is God who is at work in us through the Holy Spirit. Imitation is part of the process. We expend effort. But ultimately God is the artist who not only guides the pen but provides the strength and skill.

REST IS A PLACE

The author of Hebrews speaks of God's rest as a destination or location. He calls it "his" (God's) rest but also says it is a rest we "enter" and warns that it is possible to "fall short" of it (Heb 4:1). This imagery is drawn from God's promise to provide a place of rest for Israel after the exodus from Egypt. Before rest is a practice, it is an experience. Before we can engage in rest as a discipline we must first receive it as a gift from God.

Because we are activists by nature, we would prefer to begin with technique. We want to know what methods will enable us to experience rest. Rest seems like it should be a matter of rhythm, balance and measured effort. In other words, we think of rest as something we must do. It is just another kind of work or a different way of doing our work. But the experience of God's rest begins with something that has been done for us. The lesson of Genesis is that the first work of rest is to cease from our own effort. All that needs to be done has already been done. The work of God was finished long before we ever came on the scene. The first move for those who hope to work at rest is to recognize its passive nature. Rest is something we receive. Those who enter into God's rest recognize that rest is something God grants to us. It is grounded on work only God can do. Rest begins with God; it does not begin with us.

But if rest is a country, it is not our native country. Like the land promised to ancient Israel, it is ours only after we receive it from God as a gift and an inheritance (Lev 20:24). The generation that left Egypt failed to enter the land because they did not believe God's promise. Even when Joshua led the second generation into Canaan, they did not find the rest promised (Heb 4:8). This means that the promise of rest is still open.

Like Israel we experience divine rest starting with relocation. We must be transferred out of the dominion of darkness, which is our natural domain, and into the kingdom of Christ (Col 1:12-13). Instead of relocating to a different point on the map we are brought into union with Christ. According to Ephesians 2:6, God has raised us up with Christ and seated us with him in the heavenly realms. John Stott notes that there is more to this description than mysticism: "It bears witness to a living experience, that Christ has given us on the one hand a new life (with sensitive awareness of the reality of God, and a love for him and for his people) and on the other a new victory (with evil increasingly under our feet)."[2]

Without this change of venue we would forever remain aliens when it comes to God's kingdom. Apart from the grace of Christ we are alienated from God because of sin and are by nature the objects of his wrath. Because we do not share the concerns of heaven, we pursue the ways of this world and our actions further Satan's agenda of disobedience. We do not need to become Satan worshipers to accomplish this. All that is necessary is for us to follow the inclinations of our fallen nature.

In Romans 7 the apostle Paul paints a graphic portrait of what such a life is like. Even when we agree that the commands of God's Word are good, we often find that we cannot follow through on our determination to obey them. Something deep within subverts our good intentions. Sin is so deeply entrenched in us that it can override our genuine desire to obey God. Therefore if it is to provide real rest, transference into Christ's kingdom must do more than provide us with a new identity as a citizen of the kingdom. There must also be a corresponding change in our nature.

There are several important biblical words that describe the extent of this change. The most comprehensive is the word "salvation." Salvation expresses the sum of all that God has done, is doing and will do for us through Jesus Christ. Jesus himself used the word to describe his mission (Lk 19:10). Salvation is God's gift given to those who have faith in Christ. It cannot be earned. Because of its comprehensive nature, many of the things that can be said about salvation also apply to the other terms.

Another important word that helps us to understand our experience is "redemption." To be redeemed is to be saved. However, the idea of redemption emphasizes the notion of ransom or exchange. Redemption is God's work through Christ's sacrificial death, which provided forgiveness for sin and real righteousness for those who believe. Redemption requires Christ to act on our behalf. We do not redeem ourselves. Jesus implied as much when he characterized his mission as one of providing a "ransom for many" (Mt 20:28; Mk 10:45; see also 1 Tim 2:6). Those who are redeemed by Christ enter into God's rest by ceasing from their own efforts to gain righteousness and by relying on the work that Jesus has already accomplished on their behalf. He is "the Lamb that was slain from the creation of the world" (Rev 13:8).

When God redeems us he does more than give us the right

to enter heaven's precincts. He makes us fit for heaven. The change we experience in redemption is immediate but the full effect is not. Redemption begins with God's declaration that we have been made righteous by the blood of Christ shed as a sacrifice of atonement. In this respect it is an accomplished fact and is spoken of in Scripture in the past tense. Redemption is already in our possession. But the experience of redemption is also ongoing. The Holy Spirit is presently carrying out a ministry of transformation in those who are redeemed by Christ. His presence introduces a new operating principle within that enables us to overrule the inclinations of the fallen nature (Rom 8:2-9).

The term that is sometimes used to refer to this process is "sanctification," which is really just a form of the word "holy." To be sanctified is to be made holy. Like salvation and redemption, sanctification can be understood both as a state and a process. Since believers have already been declared righteous by God, the believer's holiness is sometimes spoken of in Scripture as if it were already an accomplished fact. "Saint" or "holy one" is the title the Bible uses to refer to those who belong to Christ. Sanctification is also a progressive work of the Spirit. We grow because of God's grace but that growth in grace is gradual. The Holy Spirit's presence is our guarantee that God will finish the work he has begun.

> Rest is a practice because the "work" of rest is rooted in the finished work of God.

All of this is part of the rest of God. Rest is a practice because the "work" of rest is rooted in the finished work of God. The effort of the Christian life is energized by rest. Biblical rest does not make us passive or unproductive. It is the secret to all productivity in the Christian life. But before rest can be a practice, it must be a spiritual location. Rest is a state of being that is essential to Christian living; it is the engine that drives all Christian action. What we do for God is dependent on what God has done for us. Here is the fundamental difference between God's rest and ours: on the seventh day of creation God rested from his work. We enter this same rest when we rest in God's work.

THE PURSUIT OF REST

Although we don't usually think of rest as an activity, it is nonetheless something we pursue. After all, rest is a verb as well as a noun. But if rest is an act, it is a special kind of act. Like sleep, rest begins with surrender. When we rest we relinquish control of the world and resign ourselves to be carried along by a current that has already been set in motion. When it comes to spiritual rest, this is a current that has been set in motion by God himself. Rest also requires a measure of trust. We lie down and close our eyes in sleep because we believe that the world will get along fine without us for a time. God will take care of us and the world during our slumber. As the Psalmist declares, "I lie down and sleep; I wake again, because the LORD sustains me" (Ps 3:5). When we rest we disengage from normal activity, confident that the things that concern us will move forward even without the effort of our hand. This makes rest an exercise in faith.

Certainly there are steps we can take to put us in a better position to experience rest. We can find a place of solitude or turn off the cell phone. We can abstain from social media or even take refuge in a cave in the wilderness. But these measures do not in themselves cause the rest we seek. Rest is something that comes to us "not without our own efforts but nevertheless not through those efforts."[3] Rest overtakes us the way that sleep does. We arrange our schedule or structure our environment so that we can wait for it, but even our best measures sometimes fail us. We might find that we feel just as harried in our place of solitude as we did in the thick of our daily work. We can leave our job behind only to discover that we are still plagued by worries about it.

Consequently, there is more to pursuing rest than selecting the right method. The concrete steps we take to prepare for rest and the disciplines we practice (like observing Sabbath as a regular discipline) are ways that we reposition ourselves so that we are more susceptible to rest. But resting is not itself rest any more than eating is food.

Rest is a standing. It is a state or condition into which we enter and in which we remain. We sometimes speak of an object as being "at rest." The same can be said of us. There is a positional dimension to the rest we enjoy in Christ. We see this reflected in the language the Bible uses to speak of our relationship to Christ. We are described as being "in" Christ. We have been rescued out of the domain of darkness and have been "brought into" the kingdom of the Father's beloved Son (Col 1:12). As a result the Scriptures describe our present position as one in which we are already seated with Christ in the heavenly realms (Eph 2:6). When we are united to Christ by faith, we enter into his finished work. All that needs to be done to reconcile us to God has been done. We did not create this rest nor can we add anything to it. Like the land that was promised to Israel, the rest Christ provides is both our permanent possession and our proper location. Rest in this sense is a domain out of which we operate.

But rest is also a practice—one with which action is not incompatible. Those who enter the rest of Christ cease from their own works but they do not cease to work. Just as the Father is both always at rest and always at his work, we have been "created in Christ Jesus to do good works, which God prepared in advance for us to do" (Eph 2:10). The Greek text says that we would "walk in them." These are works that God has planned for us and for which he empowers us. This means the domain of rest is also a realm of activity. When we work at rest we also work out of a state of rest. We recognize that the good works God has planned for us proceed from the finished work of Christ. The things we do are not additions to or substitutions for all that Jesus has done on our behalf. They are an extension of his work in us. Rest is a way of life.

Sleep is a form of rest but not all rest is sleep. God rested on the seventh day but never sleeps. Physical rest comes to us when we yield to our weariness but God never grows weary. He offers himself to us as a place of repose. He prepares the work we are to do and provides the energy we need to accomplish it. Because he has invited us into his rest, he also commands us to wake up and walk in the light of Christ. Stay awake!

QUESTIONS FOR REFLECTION

1. What is the "rest of God"? How does this phrase describe God himself? How does it describe something God provides? Is the notion of a God who rests comforting or troublesome to you? Why?

2. What does it imply about God to say that he is still at rest? Does this mean God is detached and disinterested in creation? Is rest incompatible with activity? Why or why not?

3. How does God's rest differ from ours? In what ways does our experience of rest depend on God's rest?

4. How would you explain the relationship between rest and righteousness? Can you have righteousness without rest? Can you have rest without righteousness?

5. In what sense is rest a state of being? In what sense is it a location? In what sense is it a person?

BEYOND *the*
DAY *of* REST

My earliest notion of Sabbath was shaped by Sunday, a day infused with equal measures of tedium and dread. We did not call Sunday the Sabbath in our unchurched home. Sunday was merely a day off. Yet even though Sunday arrived in company with Saturday, it was easy to tell that the two were not the same. Sunday was Saturday's grave companion. On Sunday everything seemed different: the television we watched, the food we ate and even the way we played. All were altered by the nature of the day.

In the morning I turned on the television to find the cartoons I loved so much on Saturday replaced by more serious fare. I clicked through the channels and listened as the drone of newscasters mingled with the shout of a brow-mopping faith healer and the low hum of the priest who chanted the Mass for the sick and shut-in. I listened to their strange antiphony with morbid fascination. How sick were the people who went down at the touch and cry of the faith healer? Who were these shut-ins and what was the priest saying to them? It seemed to me that the faith healer was doing something on an entirely different order than the priest. There was something vaguely oppressive about both to me, though I would not have been able to tell you why.

Outside the street was deserted. The friends I had played with the day before were nowhere to be found. They were either squirming in solemn discomfort on the hard pews of the Catholic church down the street or seated next to their grandparents at ordinary tables now dignified by the elegance of Sunday china. Dinners were different at our house too when Sunday came. The common fare we ate during the week was replaced with the kind of food that took hours to cook and filled the house with its aroma—a joy when the main course was beef and a torment when the dish included sauerkraut.

On Sunday my parents picked up the leftover debris of Saturday, both literally and figuratively. Occasionally they entertained on Saturdays, filling the night with the mysterious sound of clinking glasses, food that I could not share and adult conversation. Sometimes they went out and came home late. But most Saturday evenings they just sat in front of the television while my mother sipped her beer and my father drank his vodka. In the secret heart of the night I could hear strange sounds emanating from their bedroom. This was the noise of passion and sometimes of anger. They slept late the next day emerging bleary-eyed and tentative, like those who find themselves on new terrain and are unsure of their surroundings.

I came to see Sunday as a day off like Saturday but without the enthusiasm. The sense of leisure that filled the house on Saturday evaporated by Sunday evening, leached away by dissipation and the dull approach of Monday. This was how the weekend always ended in our house. Sunday evenings were tinged with regret, crowned by a general sense of apprehension for the coming week. Chronologically speaking, Sunday may have been the first day of the week for some. But to me Sunday always seemed to represent the collapse of the weekend.

The character of Sunday changed a little when I began to follow Christ. Yet not as much as you might think. Now that I belonged to Christ I felt that Sunday should be the most important day of my week. My Sundays were devoted to worship and socializing with my friends at church. The socializing was often more interesting than the worship, especially when I was dating. When I became a pastor, Sunday also became the focal point of my workweek. On that day all the labor I had poured into prayer and study of the Word during the prior six days found its expression. I was convinced that Sunday was the most important day of the week for my congregation, especially the hour or so they spent listening to me.

Yet I was dismayed to learn that they did not always share my estimation of the day. They made church a priority, for the most part. That is to say, they showed up week after week and listened politely as I declaimed to them about their souls. But I quickly learned that Sunday was important to the congregation for other things besides church. Sunday was the day they watched their children play baseball or soccer, which sometimes required them to skip church. They took short vacations on the weekend that overlapped with the day of worship. They left the service early to celebrate birthdays, prepare dinner for their extended family or attend picnics.

To be honest, I resented these liberties. I told myself that this kind of behavior betrayed a lack of commitment. After all, how could these people love Jesus above all else if they could not remain focused on him for even one day a week?

After I left the pastorate and became a college professor, it occurred to me that the resentment I felt was as much a result of my own ambition and pride as it was an expression of priestly concern for their souls. Like a cook who has labored over an extravagant meal only to find that those for whom it has been prepared aren't hungry, I took congregational absences and early departures personally. I wondered how the church would ever grow into the large congregation I wanted it to become with such inconsistent attendance. I suspect that there was also a touch of jealousy in my response. After all, church was my job. I couldn't skip the service even if I had wanted to. On long weekends, when members of my congregation left town or visited their relatives, I had to remain and go to church.

I cannot help noticing (and envying) the difference in Susannah Heschel's description of her experience of the Jewish Shabbat while growing up. Heschel writes that Friday evening, the beginning of the Jewish Sabbath, was the climax of the week. As she and her mother lit the Sabbath candles, she felt transformed both emotionally and physically. "The sense of peace that came upon us as we kindled the lights was created, in part, by the hectic tension of Fridays," Heschel explains. "Preparation for a holy day, my father often said, was as important as the day itself."[1] In reflection, what seems clear to me about my Sunday experience is that rest did not figure into it at all. Not for me or for anyone else I knew.

THE CHURCH AND THE SABBATH

The church has never been uniform in its conviction about the Sabbath or its practice. In his study of the cultural transformation of Sunday, Stephen Miller notes that Sunday observance was an important issue in late antiquity and in Britain and

America from about 1600 to 1950.[2] Miller observes that it was the subject of forty-seven acts of Parliament and was often debated by American legislators in the nineteenth and early twentieth centuries. The roots of this debate go back even further. According to Richard Bauckham the early church was itself divided on the issue. Bauckham notes, "The early church had no single answer to the question of the relevance of the Sabbath commandment to Christians. The churches of the New Testament period included a variety of views."[3]

Like my parents, most people today consider Sunday to be part of the weekend. The first day of the week is just a day off, and for some it is not even that. Those who still have the luxury of treating Sunday as a day of leisure do not find much occasion to rest on it. Our notion of rest has become commingled with play, and in many cases our

> Sunday observance of the Sabbath was the subject of forty-seven acts of Parliament and often debated by American legislators in the nineteenth and early twentieth centuries.

play is as arduous as our work. Who has not returned to the workplace on Monday only to hear coworkers complain that they need another day off to recover from the weekend?

Few Christians today treat Sunday as the Sabbath. Some do not even think it is distinctive as a day of worship. They prefer to worship in the middle of the week or on Friday or Saturday. The church has few sacred days left. Even Christmas and Easter might be more accurately described as holidays rather than holy days. The notion of a weekly observance in which one day of the week is set apart and treated as more sacred than the rest seems like a relic of the past.

The apostle Paul warned the Colossians not to let anyone

judge them when it came to religious festivals, new moon celebrations or Sabbath days (Col 2:16). These were all associated with the Mosaic Law. Certainly New Testament believers were not required to forswear the observance of all sacred days. Paul's own practice after his conversion to Christ was to visit the synagogue on the Sabbath. However, this seems to have been driven more by evangelistic intent than by any continued devotion to the day itself. On the first day of the week Paul gathered with other Christians for worship, the regular practice of the New Testament church.

Worship on the first day instead of the seventh differentiated Christian custom from Jewish, but the selection of the day itself was the result of its association with the resurrection of Jesus Christ rather than a reaction against the Jews or the Sabbath itself. The first day of the week became the "Lord's Day" in the nomenclature of the church (Rev 1:10). A similar construction is used in 1 Corinthians 11:20 to speak of communion, which Paul refers to as the "Lord's Supper." This is fitting since it was on the Lord's Day that the church met to partake of the Lord's Supper. But Sunday was not the only day when the early church gathered. In Jerusalem the church engaged in a daily distribution to the widows of the congregation (Acts 6:1). The believers in Jerusalem also met daily in the temple courts and in their homes (Acts 2:46). At this early stage the apostles continued to observe the worship rhythms of their Jewish tradition (Acts 3:1).[4]

Some Christians continue to call Sunday the Sabbath as a matter of tradition. It is the church's sacred day. Yet it seems clear that certain features of Israel's Sabbath practice on the seventh day set it apart from Christian observance of the first day of the week. The Lord's Day was never encumbered with the kind of limitations that were typical of the Hebrew Sabbath. All work was forbidden on the Sabbath except for the labor required for the preparation of meals. During their journey through the wilderness people could not even gather manna on the seventh day. Instead God's people were confined to quarters. Contemporary readers who stumble upon these Sabbath restrictions in the Old Testament might find it hard to imagine that anyone would have welcomed them. In the Law of Moses the weekly observance of Sabbath was framed as a reminder of Israel's liberation from slavery. To the modern reader it seems like the opposite. The limitations set on personal behavior feel confining in the worst sense of the word. These restrictions sound rigid to the modern ear, hardly conducive to the experience of rest.

The gravity of the day was underscored early in Israel's experience when a man who gathered wood on the Sabbath was arrested, placed in custody and then executed (Num 15:32-36). The austere requirements surrounding the day combined with such stark enforcement make contemporary appeals to the Sabbath "principle" seem a bit romanticized. To the modern ear the voice of the Sabbath sounds stern and parental at best. It is as if God were saying, "Go to your room." At worst, it seems inflexible and perhaps even abusive. As if the true message of the Sabbath was "Rest or I'll kill you."

Israel's observance of the seventh day was more than a spiritual practice. It was primarily a covenant sign. In Exodus 31:17 the Lord calls the Sabbath "a sign between me and the Israelites forever." Israel was commanded to treat the seventh day differently than the surrounding nations did. When Israel kept the seventh day holy, they bore witness to their unique status as God's chosen people. This covenant obligation was combined with social function. By declaring the day to be sacred, the Lord invested it with the power to reach deep into every level of society. Son and daughter, manservant and maidservant, native citizens, aliens and even animals were bound by it. The restrictions placed on activity represented liberation from toil for those who had no control over their own labor.

The practice of Sabbath also had a profound effect on Israel's economic and ecological practices. In addition to the weekly Sabbath, every seven years God's people observed a Sabbath year during which the land was left fallow and debts were canceled. Every fifty years Israel celebrated the year of Jubilee. Fields were to remain unplanted and vineyards untended. During this heightened Sabbath year indentured servants were given their freedom and family property that had been sold, probably out of financial exigency, reverted to its original owner. As a social institution, Israel's Sabbath observance provided rest for the land and economic protection for the community as a whole. The prophets mixed divine reproofs for failing to keep the Sabbath law with social rebuke for ignoring the plight of the poor. Abuse of one led to exploitation of the other.

> The prophets mixed divine reproofs for failing to keep the Sabbath law with social rebuke for ignoring the plight of the poor. Abuse of one led to exploitation of the other.

What should Christians make of the Sabbath today? Some view the biblical Sabbath primarily as social commentary. For them it represents God's vote cast in favor of the poor. In the institution of the Sabbath, especially in its more extensive forms, they see a justification for economic restructuring, redistribution of wealth and evidence of divine advocacy for justice. Richard

Lowery reflects this view when he says, "Biblical sabbath and jubilee traditions provide a lens by which to focus theological reflection on the spiritual, ecological, and economic challenges that face us in this era of globalizing economy."[5]

However, viewing the Sabbath only as a socioeconomic structure binds it so closely to the cultural and economic context of ancient Israel that it becomes irrelevant for us today. It is doubtful that we would be able to implement the structures of the Sabbath into today's economy even if we wanted to. Such a perspective risks reducing the Sabbath to a bumper sticker that reminds us to drop a coin in the cup of the nearest beggar we pass on the way to work.

Others approach the Sabbath in spiritualized and individualistic terms. Their practice has more in common with someone who takes up running or weightlifting than with those who were required to observe the Sabbath as a matter of law. One person spends the day engaging in worship, prayer and Bible reading, while another uses it as a day to relax. Although some feel that the very idea of Sabbath practice is bound up with congregational worship, many do not see a need to include the church in their Sabbath observance. For more than a few, the practice of "Sabbath" is indistinguishable from what others call a "day off." This individualized approach is more practical but tends to privatize the biblical Sabbath and ignores its larger implications.

The biblical observance of Sabbath was an obligation under the Law of Moses. Now that Christ has come things have changed. Israel looked forward to a promise that was yet to come. We look back to a promise that has been fulfilled. According to Colossians 2:17, Christ is the "reality" of all that the biblical Sabbath represented. Perhaps this is why the first day

eventually replaced the seventh in the life of the church. The
Sabbath foreshadowed; the Lord's Day memorializes. We can
still practice Sabbath as a discipline. Such a practice is a matter
of what we do as much as it is a function of what we do not do.

Dallas Willard observes, "In the simplest possible terms, the
spiritual disciplines are a matter of taking appropriate measures."[6] We take appropriate measures when we practice Sabbath
as a discipline by introducing a different rhythm into our
schedule. We set aside a regular time to pursue rest. We clear
our schedule. We turn off the phone and the computer in order
to silence their constant demands for our attention. We abstain
from our ordinary and necessary work. We may even arrange our
surroundings or remove ourselves to another location for a time.
The aim of all this effort is to create an atmosphere that will
allow space for God. Or, more accurately, our aim is to create a
climate that allows space for our own awareness of God. God is
always present with us. It is our preoccupation with the necessities of life that often distract us from him.

BEYOND THE DAY OF REST

But rest is more than a spiritual discipline and the Sabbath is
more than a day. In the Law of Moses, observance of the Sabbath
was a moral and a social obligation that pointed to something
greater than itself. Theologian Geerhardus Vos calls the biblical
Sabbath an eschatological sign. "The Sabbath is not in the first
place a means of advancing religion," Vos explains. "It has its
major significance apart from that, in pointing forward to the
eternal issues of life and history."[7] In the Law of Moses the
Sabbath was a concrete expression of God's rule over his people.
By it they experienced his provision for them. By keeping the
Sabbath in all its forms, the people of Israel were reminded that

they were dependent on God and interconnected with each other. Israel's Sabbath experience was an experiential signpost woven into the fabric of their common life that pointed to the rest of God. This is something God's people would later come to know as the kingdom.

These Sabbath laws made God's people acutely aware of their weak faith. This deficiency is reflected in the question raised in connection with the year of Jubilee in Leviticus 25:20: "You may ask, 'What will we eat in the seventh year if we do not plant or harvest our crops?'" God's answer to their question is as expansive in its generosity as it is in its expectation of faith: "I will send you such a blessing in the sixth year that the land will yield enough for three years. While you plant during the eighth year, you will eat from the old crop and will continue to eat from it until the harvest of the ninth year comes in" (Lev 25:21-22).

We can hear in this reply a foreshadowing of Jesus' admonition to his disciples to seek the kingdom in Matthew 6:31-33: "So do not worry, saying, 'What shall we eat?' or 'What shall we drink?' or 'What shall we wear?' For the pagans run after all these things, and your heavenly Father knows that you need them. But seek first his kingdom and his righteousness, and all these things will be given to you as well." Jesus' promise must have seemed equally improbable to the disciples. It addresses the same question Israel asked regarding the year of Jubilee: "If we do as you say, what will we eat?"

This was not a trivial question. It is all the more reasonable when we consider that the year of Jubilee required Israel to forgo the normal means of production used by God to provide for his people. Planting and harvesting were not presumptuous acts. Nor were they expressions of independence from God. It was God himself who established the pattern of sowing and reaping that produced the harvest. The regular cycle of seedtime and harvest were marks of his faithfulness. Sin had introduced a dimension of painful toil into the process, but the work itself was part of creation's order. Israel lived by a rule that God himself established and that still abides today. If we do not work, we do not eat (see 2 Thess 3:10). Consequently, God's promise to provide so extravagantly in the sixth year was much more than a test of Israel's faith. It was a foretaste of the ultimate rest of a kingdom yet to come. In the same way, Jesus' command to seek the kingdom first points to a divine economy that is radically unlike the one we normally operate within.

The Old Testament Sabbath in its various forms deliberately upset the equilibrium of the ordinary world by interjecting into it the order of the world to come. Jesus does the same in Matthew 6:31-33 when he urges us to give the kingdom of God priority over food, drink and clothing. His appeal is an invitation to rest as much as it is an admonition to seek. After all, what do food, drink and clothing have to do with the kingdom? Why should seeking such things necessarily preclude the kingdom? This is comparing apples and oranges. The anxiety we feel about our daily necessities is born of experience. The past has shown that normally we must procure these things for ourselves. Jesus is certainly making a value statement when he urges us to make the kingdom our priority. The Father's kingdom and its attendant righteousness are worth more than our necessary food. But he is also making a point about the way God works. The kingdom is not of our own making and neither are the things that seem to come from our own hand. God provides them all. By redirecting our attention to the kingdom, Jesus offers a balm for our ordinary anxiety. If God is able to provide us with a kingdom, how much easier is it for him to supply us with food and drink? If he has covered us with his righteousness, will he not also cover our bodies with clothing? It is God who ultimately supplies what we need. Even when we seem to procure our own food and clothing, we are really receiving these things as a gift from the Father's hand.

To seek first the Father's kingdom and his righteousness means that we will make the kingdom and righteousness our priority. But it also means that we will rest, because to seek is to trust. The Father who is "pleased to give you the kingdom" is just as pleased to provide our food and clothing (Lk 12:32). Food and clothing turn out to be emblems of all we receive from God. With such reassuring words Christ transforms our daily necessities into signs of the kingdom. Hunger and thirst point to our need. The satisfaction we feel after we have eaten and drunk is a token of his grace. No wonder Jesus chose food and drink as the chief emblems of the grace he bestows on the church. It is also no wonder that when Jesus taught the church to pray, he taught us to pray for daily bread along with the coming of the kingdom. These small requests along with their answers are "a crack in the door" that offers "a glimpse of the festal hall of the Father's house and your eternal home."[8]

The writer of Hebrews describes Sabbath both as a location and as a state of being by linking the believer's experience with the promise of rest made to Israel and with the rest of God described in Genesis. Those who believe in Christ relocate. They enter a rest withheld from those not allowed to enter Canaan (Heb 4:3). They also change their state of being. Those who are in Christ are at rest. They have ceased from their own works the way God did from his (Heb 4:10). In this way the writer of Hebrews captures the dual condition of those who are in Christ. They are both at rest and in motion. Believers have already entered into a state of rest by turning from their own efforts to rely on the work of Christ. At the same time they are pilgrims en route to a final rest that will come when the church's prayer for the kingdom is finally answered. To fully grasp the biblical idea of rest we must look beyond the Sabbath day and Sabbath discipline. Both point to something else. Rest is ultimately a person. When Jesus invites us to come to him, he invites us to enter his kingdom of rest.

QUESTIONS FOR REFLECTION

1. What day of the week is your favorite? What is it about this day that appeals to you?

2. Many Christians no longer treat Sunday as their primary day of worship. Do you think this matters? Do you think those who follow Jesus should regard Sunday as a Sabbath day? Why or why not?

3. Does the Old Testament practice of keeping the Sabbath seem like freedom or a restriction to you? Why do you think the New Testament believers did not treat the first day of the week the same as the Jewish people did the seventh day?

4. How did the Old Testament institution of the Sabbath anticipate the coming of the kingdom and the future rule of Christ? In what sense is Sabbath a principle? In what sense is it a state of being? In what sense is it a person?

5. What value is there in observing Sabbath as a spiritual discipline?

- 4 -

FALSE REST

In my last year of college I got a part-time job with a major automobile company as a teletype messenger. It was a dream job. I spent four hours a day delivering telegrams to the fifteen floors of the company's world headquarters in downtown Detroit. Actually, I probably spent little more than an hour and a half delivering telegrams. The rest of the time I spent chatting with the secretaries, browsing in the bookstore across the street, eating doughnuts in the coffee shop on the first floor or reading the newspaper with my coworkers in the supply room. It wasn't rocket science.

One week as part of a self-study the company brought in an efficiency expert to observe us. He took a seat a few feet from our workstation and watched as we tore the messages off the teletype machines and addressed them. When he asked if he could accompany one of us, we sent him with Norman, who was the slowest. Counting on the fact that the expert was unfamiliar with the layout of our building, Norman meandered through his route beginning at the end and working his way slowly back to the start. He skipped several stops and then doubled back to make deliveries to them. Instead of taking the elevator, he used the stairs. When he was finally done the efficiency expert declared, "Well, you've convinced me. You need more help!"

After graduation I transferred to the mailroom and pushed a wire cart along a similar route delivering interoffice mail. I made four runs a day. In between I read magazines, listened to the radio and gossiped with my coworkers. To be honest, none of this felt much like work. One day while on my mail route, I accidently stepped onto the express elevator that was reserved for the executives. As the car began to climb, a distinguished looking man in a well-tailored suit smiled at me and asked, "Are you working hard today?" In a moment of regrettable honesty I replied, "Not really."

His smile turned frosty. "I'm sorry to hear that!" he said. I was rescued from the awkwardness of the moment when the elevator doors opened and I made a red-faced exit.

Sometimes work isn't work. I've had more than one job where a supervisor took me aside and asked me to slow down because I was making the others I worked with look bad. To be honest, this was usually during my first few days on the job, when I was trying to make an impression. I was surprised by the reproof. But what amazed me more was how easy it was to adjust my work habits to suit the company norm. It did not take long for me to become comfortable with the company standard and even to feel exhausted by it. I have also had jobs where my boss told me I wasn't working hard enough. As it turns out, I do not need organizational culture to teach me how to shirk my job. I am perfectly capable of doing this on my own.

While work isn't always work, the corollary is equally true. What passes for rest isn't always rest. The word the Bible uses when it speaks of counterfeit rest is "sloth."

Sloth is an old-fashioned word. Once considered a cardinal sin by the church, it now sounds quaint and out of step to the modern ear. Sloth seems as out of place in ordinary life as a nun's habit or a monk's cowl. We rarely use the word today. The French have a more elegant word to describe sloth. They speak of ennui—a word that refers to the dullness of spirit. Ennui begins with tedium and ends in profound disinterest. Sloth sounds gross, but ennui sounds luxurious. Perhaps it captures the languorous appeal of sloth.

Sloth is rest's dysfunctional relative. It differs in nearly every respect from true rest. Rest refreshes; sloth drains our vitality and depletes energy. Rest is a remedy; sloth is injurious. The sin of sloth is frequently conjoined with other sins in Scripture. According to Dorothy Sayers, sloth is the accomplice of all the other cardinal sins and their worst punishment: "It is the sin that believes in nothing, cares for nothing, seeks to know nothing, interferes with nothing, enjoys nothing, loves nothing, hates nothing, finds purpose in nothing, lives for nothing, and remains alive only because there is nothing it would die for."[1] Like the demon in the parable, when sloth enters the house it often brings with it seven spirits more wicked than itself. Sloth is the enemy of both work and rest.

A SIN OF OMISSION

The Hebrew word for sloth conveys the idea of laxness or slackness. Sloth is a sin of omission—a failure to do what is required, right or good. The lurid portrait that the book of Proverbs paints of this sin not only gives us a sense of sloth's effect but also hints at the kind of environment in which it develops. The slothful man may capture his game but will not bother to cook it. He buries his hand in the dish but does not have the motivation to bring the food to his lips. Sloth is the opposite of diligence. As Proverbs 10:4 puts it, "Lazy hands make a man poor, but diligent hands bring wealth." Diligence adds but sloth subtracts. The action of a slothful hand is like the work of a dull blade. It makes all the right motions but cannot cut.

Sloth is not confined to the workplace. It prowls the corridors of the church as much as it does the factory. The Corinthian church engaged in sloth when it refused to discipline one of its members who was engaged in sexual behavior "of a kind that does not occur even among pagans" (1 Cor 5:1). In their case sloth was accompanied by spiritual pride. It did not look like laziness so much as detachment. Sloth is often mistaken for tolerance, making it an agreeable companion for many other sins. Sometimes sloth may even be mistaken for grace. Sayers says, "In the world it calls itself tolerance; but in hell it is called despair."[2]

> Sloth is not confined to the workplace. It prowls the corridors of the church as much as it does the factory.

The root sin of sloth is expressed in the apostle's challenge in 1 Corinthians 5:2: "Shouldn't you rather have . . . ?" Sloth is a sin of ignored responsibility and missed opportunity. This is its real tragedy. It is also one of the reasons sloth is so easy to tolerate. The benefits of resisting sloth are invisible to us because they are confined to the realm of what "might have been." They are easily dismissed as hypothetical. We might have done better. But who can really say that things would have been different had we acted? Jesus shines a light on sloth in the parable of the talents in

Matthew 25. A master entrusted varying amounts of money to his servants before going on a journey. When he returned, he called them together to give an account. Three of the four produced a profit. But one returned exactly what had been given to him. His defense unmasks the protectionism that often gives sloth its point of entry into our lives: "Then the man who had received the one talent came. 'Master,' he said, 'I knew that you are a hard man, harvesting where you have not sown and gathering where you have not scattered seed. So I was afraid and went out and hid your talent in the ground. See, here is what belongs to you'" (Mt 25:24-25).

Instead of being pleased by such fiscal conservatism, the master was angry. He replied, "You wicked, lazy servant! So you knew that I harvest where I have not sown and gather where I have not scattered seed? Well then, you should have put my money on deposit with the bankers, so that when I returned I would have received it back with interest" (Mt 25:26-27). The master's criticism calls the servant's judgment into question. If he really was such a hard man, why didn't the servant take steps to guarantee a return? Was it fear or apathy that kept the servant from doing what he should? Sometimes it's hard to tell the two apart. What looks like apathy may also be a byproduct of fear.

This was true of Israel when they failed to enter Canaan under Moses' leadership. They panicked when they heard that the people of Canaan were powerful, the cities fortified and the land filled with giants. They were daunted by the size of the task. Yet Israel's root misconception had to do with God. "If only we had died in Egypt! Or in this desert!" they complained in Numbers 14:2-3. "Why is the LORD bringing us to this land only to let us fall by the sword? Our wives and children will be taken as plunder. Wouldn't it be better for us to go back to Egypt?" Despite God's promises, they concluded that he hated them and was bent on their destruction. Sloth may not turn us into atheists in the technical sense, but it does make practical atheists of us. Even when we continue to believe in God's existence and power, we lose confidence in his willingness to act on our behalf. This means sloth is more a failure of faith than the onset of laziness. We have no taste for the challenge before us because we have lost sight of God's goodness.

Since sloth often involves a failure to act when we should, we might assume that action is the first step toward recovery. But this isn't always the case. When Israel balked at the prospect of entering Canaan, they attempted to repair their sin by taking action. They only failed again. As important as the task was, Israel's relationship with God was even more important. When it comes to dealing with sloth, it is our vision of God that must be mended even more than our actions. The first step in recovering from this sin is to realign our vision of God so that we can clearly see where he stands in relation to us and fully reorient our behavior. Without a proper view of God any action we take will provide only temporary relief from sloth—if it provides relief at all. Consequently, the remedy for sloth is ultimately a matter of resting in God.

This was Israel's root problem when they failed to act on the border of Canaan. The same was also true when they tried to enter Canaan against God's will. Both their initial failure to act and their subsequent rash attempt to obey (which was really a form of disobedience) reflected a lack of faith. Rest requires that we trust that God is still for us, even when he asks us to live with the consequences of our own disobedience. If sloth is a failure to trust and to act, it is also a failure to wait. We are most tempted to succumb to sloth when we grow weary of waiting for God to show up. Consequently, sloth does not always make us sleepy. Sometimes it makes us agitated. The sin of sloth is just as likely to manifest itself in anxiety as in lethargy. The ancients called sloth "the noonday demon" that makes the day drag and disquiets the soul. Sloth thrives in an atmosphere of boredom. Sayers writes that "it is one of the favorite tricks of this sin to dissemble itself under cover of a whiffling activity of body. We think that if we are busily rushing about and doing things, we cannot be suffering from sloth."[3]

THE EFFECT OF SLOTH ON PRAYER

Because sloth is a spiritual malady it insinuates itself into our spiritual practices. The practice of prayer is one of the most common arenas where I do battle with sloth. Sometimes, like the disciples in the garden, I find that sloth manifests itself as lethargy. I set out to pray but my mind wanders and I soon become drowsy. I begin with prayer and before I know it I am dreaming. I sleep because I am bored. My prayer seems to be little more than a monologue at best or a grocery list at worst. I do not see how it can be very interesting to God. It is barely of interest to me.

At other times the noonday demon appears in a less languid form. I try to pray but I am distracted by my work or my ministry. Even as I speak to God, the necessities of life rush in to crowd him out of my thinking. My contemplation of God quickly gives way to busy planning and then to activity.

The truth is, I am more comfortable working than I am praying. Work seems to garner quicker results. Work is familiar territory for me. When I am in the place of work, I know what to say and what to do. Prayer, on the other hand, seems more like a series of awkward conversations and long silences. I do not always feel like God is listening to me. It does not seem like anything is getting done. Of course, there is a place for work— there are even times when it is better to act than to pray. When Israel saw the Egyptians marching after them they prayed. God's surprising response was to call them to action. The Lord said to Moses, "Why are you crying out to me? Tell the Israelites to move on" (Ex 14:15). But prayer allows us to take up the task assigned to us by God from a position of rest. Prayer introduces a relational dimension to our work. It reminds us that we are not merely working for God; we also belong to him.

However, while prayer may be our first work, it is not our only work. We are not monks. We have jobs, families and busy commutes. Most of us do not have the luxury of devoting our day exclusively to prayer. We may not even have the liberty of controlling our day. We answer to others and have people who depend on us. We cannot do only as we please, even when it comes to finding time to pray. It often seems that all we have left are the "crumbs of wasted time."[4] We wanted to offer God the first fruits of our day but find that he must be satisfied with the leavings instead.

Archbishop Anthony Bloom points to a better way. The solution to both the boredom and the agitation that afflict us in prayer is the way of rest. Bloom notes that we can pray to God only if we are established in a state of stability and inner peace as we are face to face with God. This sense of peace and stability will not add minutes to our day. But it will release us from the sense that we are running out of time or that time is dragging on as the world rushes past us. One way we do this is by learning how to establish ourselves in the present. This is something we can do in those scattered moments when we have nothing to do. We sit down, relax and consciously make ourselves aware of the present, of ourselves and of God. One reason we so easily yield to sloth during prayer is that we do not feel a sense of God's presence. In reality it is we who are absent. Another reason is that we think the world cannot get along without us. We are uncomfortable during prayer. We do not feel like we are very good at it. While we struggle, precious time seems to be slipping away, along with the opportunities it provides to accomplish our goals.

Bloom suggests that we combat this by talking to ourselves during those moments when we have nothing to do: "You sit down and say 'I am seated, I am doing nothing, I will do nothing for five minutes,' and then relax, and continually throughout this time (one or two minutes is the most you will be able to endure to begin with) realize, 'I am here in the presence of God, in my own presence and in the presence of all the furniture that is around me, just still, going nowhere.'"[5] After we learn how to do this for brief periods of time we can expand it to greater lengths and eventually to situations when we are busy. We will find that the world will survive without us during these moments of rest. Bloom assures, "Learn to master time, and you will be able—whatever you do, whatever the stress, in the storm, in tragedy, or simply in the confusion in which we continuously live—to be still, immobile in the present, face to face with the Lord, in silence or in words."[6]

SLOTH DISGUISED AS VISION

Again, sloth does not always lead to lethargy. Often it lends itself to fantasizing and bad planning. This makes sloth a breeding ground for ill-conceived shortcuts, unproductive tangents and unnecessary distractions. When we give in to sloth, we often find that we are busier than ever but busy about the wrong thing. I sometimes wonder whether the church's obsession with ministry vision is not a form of sloth. This may seem paradoxical. Vision implies action and change. Both sound like the very antithesis of sloth. But it is the impatience of sloth that disinclines us to give attention to the necessary details of our work. We do this because we have grown weary of the ordinary.

Wendell Berry's observation about farming also holds true for the life of the church. Berry observes that "one's connection to a newly bought farm will begin in love that is more or less ignorant."[7] The person who chooses to purchase it does so because he or she sees potential. "One's head, like a lover's, grows full of visions."[8] But once you buy the farm and move there, a change takes place. "Thoughts begin to be translated into acts. Truth begins to intrude with its matter-of-fact. One's work may be defined in part by visions, but it is defined in part too by problems, which the work leads to and reveals. And daily life, work, and problems gradually alter the visions."[9] Berry does not see this as the "death" of a vision but as a necessary correction. The initial vision, it turns out, was really more of an imposition. It needed the kind of refining that only sustained experience, thoughtful study and the inevitable intrusion of reality can provide.

This happens frequently in ministry. Students who feel "called" to missions after visiting another country for two weeks often sing the same refrain as pastoral candidates who spend a few days with a church they hope will offer them a position: "God gave me such a love for the people!" Each comes away from the experience with a head full of ideas, fairly swooning with the endless possibilities of ministry. But once installed, something changes. Reality combined with daily necessity intrudes on the initial vision and modifies it. The earlier image of "what might be" is limited by the constraint of "what is." Meanwhile the path to turning this corrected vision into reality proves to be a long one, made up of modest steps and commonplace effort. The initial vision was glorious but the route to fulfillment is not. It is just a regular road that does not look or feel much different than any other. Before long the commonplace scenery of ministry grows tiresome, along with its familiar tasks. It is sloth that tempts those who have grown weary with the mundane to dwell on fantasies.

True visionary leadership is a function of time, discipline and attending to the ordinary as much as it is a function of a leader's big idea. Time and discipline in particular are required because "correct discipline cannot be hurried, for it is both the knowledge of what ought to be done, and the willingness to do it—all of it, properly. One must stay to experience and study and understand the consequences—must understand them by living with them, and then correct them, if necessary, by longer living and more work."[10] The fundamentals of ministry, like the fundamentals of most vocations, are made up of daily routines that are mostly unremarkable.

This means that the context in which ministry takes place is mostly the ordinary. Eugene Peterson notes that there is a tendency to idealize ministry. "Anyone who glamorizes congregations does a grave disservice to pastors," he warns. "We hear tales of glitzy, enthusiastic churches and wonder what in the world we are doing wrong that our people don't turn out that way under our preaching. On close examination, though, it turns out that there are no wonderful congregations. Hang around long enough and sure enough there are gossips who won't shut up, furnaces that malfunction, sermons that misfire, disciples who quit, choirs who go flat—and worse."[11]

Coming to grips with this reality is one of the first major adjustments of ministry. It is not unlike what happens in some marriages after the glitter of the wedding has been swept up and the last sunset of the honeymoon week has faded from the horizon. Suddenly the couple wake up together on Monday morning without the improvements of makeup or fancy dress and find that they must go to work. Pastors who fail to adjust to reality become infatuated with a false image of ministry. Instead of accepting the church as it is, they pursue a fantasy. In some cases this leads to a gypsy life, moving from one short tenure to another in search of their dream ministry. Others stay in place but communicate their disappointment through "prophetic" preaching. This often sounds more like the scolding of a parent who is perpetually dissatisfied with their child's performance in school.

The congregation has different dreams, but its ministry expectations can be equally unrealistic. If pastors dream of elegant ministry structures, congregations fantasize about omnicompetent pastors. They want good preaching from someone who has a dynamic but approachable personality. Visions of someone who is a skilled administrator and who can combine evangelistic zeal with a compassionate bedside manner are only the start of this fantasy. Many are dreaming of the same elegant ministry structures that their pastors fantasize about. They want the services of a large church without losing the family atmosphere of the small church. Some are looking for a Moses to lead them out of the current wilderness and bring them into the land of promise. This is a land that looks suspiciously like the church as it was twenty, thirty or even fifty years ago. Or else their promised land looks curiously like the "successful" church across town.

None of these desires is necessarily sinful. But unless they are tempered by biblically informed realism, they can lead to the distraction or despair which are so characteristic of sloth.

SLOTH IS A WASTER

In my life the noonday demon of sloth has a voice. It sounds like the chime that tells me I have a new email message or that a fresh post from one of my friends has just appeared on social media. Pavlov trained his dogs to salivate at the ring of a bell. For me the sound is an invitation to click away from work or prayer and see what is going on in the virtual world. Email and social media have their place. They help me accomplish my job and enable me to stay in touch with friends who are far away. But I have learned by experience that they are just as liable to be a time waster. I scroll through the posts, reading the comments or looking at videos, and before I know it an hour has passed. My work is no further along. What is worse, I am not any better off for the time spent. Little has been said that I really care about. How many cute animal videos do I really need to watch in one day? The fact that I log on to the Internet is not what causes me to be slothful. But when I give myself up to sloth it becomes a ready tool in his hand. Nobody knows how to waste my time like the demon of sloth.

> In my life the noonday demon of sloth has a voice. It sounds like the chime that tells me I have a new email message or that a fresh post from one of my friends has just appeared on social media.

Sloth is to rest what junk food is to a nourishing meal. Despite its false promise of refreshment, sloth cannot restore us. It dissipates and leaves us spent. Even when it simulates action with all the "whiffling activity" that can attend it, sloth leaves us little to show for our effort. Sloth distracts us from God and diverts us from our legitimate work. It is a thief and a profligate. It squanders all the time, energy and affection we bestow on it. It is this wasting nature that makes sloth such a grave sin. There is a time and a place for doing nothing. But sloth is always occupied with nothing and leaves us with nothing when we are finished with it.

Our tendency to think of sloth as a minor sin from a bygone era blinds us to its ravaging nature. When we imagine a slothful person we picture someone who is fat and sluggish. But in reality the noonday demon is an emaciated spirit with a voracious appetite that is never satisfied. It consumes all that is put into its hand. It causes us to loath where we are and abhor what we are doing. It trivializes all it touches. Sloth leaches away the opportunities we have to commune with God, offering its own companionship as an anemic substitute.

It is tempting to think that the best remedy for sloth is simply to work. If we try harder we will eventually overcome. But the answer to our problem is not to be found in applying more effort. We need a different kind of effort. We will never defeat the noonday demon by work alone. The solution is to work at rest by rejecting sloth and turning to God himself.

QUESTIONS FOR REFLECTION

1. When do you feel "lazy"? What do you do (or fail to do) when you feel lazy? Do you ever feel guilty about it? Should you? Why or why not? Do you think sloth and laziness the same?

2. The church has traditionally considered sloth to be one of the seven "deadly" sins. Does the church still view sloth this

way? Do most Christians seem concerned about sloth? Why do you think this is?

3. We usually think sloth affects our view of work. In what ways can sloth ultimately be traced to our view of God? In view of this, how do we become slothful?

4. When is busyness a sign of sloth? What leads to this kind of activity? What makes it slothful?

5. In what environments are you most tempted to succumb to sloth? Are there any practical steps you can take to guard against this?

REST *and* AMBITION

A few months ago I heard a radio advertisement for a Christian university promoting its program of studies on radio and television. The tag line for the commercial was, "Be famous for God." I'm not sure which bothered me more, the naked ambition of the sentiment or the fact that it appealed to me. "You're a writer," an inner voice seemed to say. "You could be famous too!"

I only know one person who qualifies as famous. He is a millionaire, the author of a series of novels that made the *New York Times* bestseller list for several years running. He is also a serious Christian who uses his position and his wealth to advance the interests of the kingdom. But he did not set out to be famous. He is as astonished by his fame as many of his friends and family.

When we were children many of us aspired to be rock stars, NBA basketball players or famous movie actors. We may even have been told by our parents and teachers that we could achieve our goal as long as we worked hard and believed in ourselves. Perhaps they were right. In an article for the *Wall Street Journal*, author Neil Strauss observes, "Before they were famous, many of the biggest pop stars in the world believed that God wanted them to be famous, that this was his plan for them, just as it was his plan for the rest of us not to be famous. Conversely, many equally talented but slightly less famous musicians I've interviewed felt their success was accidental or undeserved—and soon after fell out of the limelight."[1]

But statistics alone reveal that fame is an unrealistic goal for the majority of people. Most who try to become movie stars, bestselling authors or professional athletes do not even make it into the profession. Among the handful that do, only a few achieve the kind of recognition that could be legitimately described as fame. We do not really expect to be famous, but we do want to be successful.

THE NATURE OF AMBITION

A few weeks after I heard the radio advertisement described above, I learned that a good friend of mine had been promoted to vice president in the organization in which we both serve. He is well-deserving of the post and in some ways the promotion was long overdue. I had prayed with him about the possibility and was genuinely pleased when it finally became a reality. Yet I confess that when I learned about it, my immediate reaction was not joy but a brief stab of irrational panic: "Everybody is getting promoted but me." This was not true, of course. Everybody was not getting promoted. My friend was and I was not. What's more, I was not even in the running for his position. I do not possess the skills or the interest to do the kind of work he does so well. So why the anxiety?

Apparently my experience is not unusual. Ambition and anxiety often go together. In his book *Status Anxiety*, author Alain de Botton calls anxiety "the handmaiden of contemporary ambition."[2] This anxiety is inevitable, de Botton explains, because the factors affecting the realization of our ambition are largely beyond our control. The measure of natural ability apportioned to me by birth, the random development of favorable circumstances in my life, whether my employer likes me, the degree of opportunity afforded by the structure of the organization, the general state of the economy—these all affect my ability to realize my ambitions. Despite the well-meaning advice we received as children, it usually takes more than belief in ourselves and hard work to become an astronaut or the president of the United States.

As somebody who is trying to engage in the radical pursuit of rest, I don't know what to do with my ambition. Most of the time I try to hide it. When somebody gives me a compliment, I usually deflect the remark. If I achieve a success of some kind, I try not to make a big deal about it. When I'm not invited to speak at the conference, my book is rejected or the score I am given by the students who evaluate my class are lower than I had hoped, I tell myself it doesn't matter. But it does. Sometimes it matters a lot. I feel disappointed. I fret. I wonder why others get noticed while I am ignored. I feel bad that I am not

> I find it hard to be at rest and ambitious at the same time.

more successful. Then I feel bad about feeling bad. I find it hard to be at rest and ambitious at the same time. Is rest really just a synonym for complacency? Should ambition even have a part in the lives of those who follow Jesus?

Before we attempt to answer these questions, we should at

least begin by admitting that we do wrestle with ambition. Ambition is no stranger to the Christian life. Believers are as ambitious as anyone else. Minimally, we would like to be at least as successful as our peers. But if we are truthful, we will admit that we would often like to do more. We would prefer to surpass them. The desire to outstrip others is felt as much by amateurs as it is by professionals. It is as true of pastors and missionaries as it is of business people. We all like to do better than somebody else.

In a memoir of his early years in pastoral ministry, Richard Lischer writes of the moment he saw the church assigned to him by his denomination after seminary. Located in a farming community in rural Illinois, Lischer put off his acceptance of the church's call because he hoped another more significant location might open up, perhaps in large city like St. Louis. The experience revealed more to Lischer about himself than it did about the church. "When you pull up to your first church, it's a moment of truth, like the first glimpse of a spouse in an arranged marriage," he writes.[3] He was dismayed when he saw the place. It was November and the drab landscape reminded him of a scene from an Ingmar Bergman film. "I felt something flop in my stomach," Lischer writes. "Then a crushing sense of disappointment. *So this is what has been prepared for me,* I thought, as if something surely *should* have been prepared for me."[4] The only thing unusual about Lischer's experience is his honesty.

When I was in seminary, I too had a mental image of the kind of church I was suited to pastor. I was not expecting to serve a megachurch. I would have been perfectly satisfied with a church of a few hundred, with a stately building and perhaps a staff member or two. During my final semester I eagerly contacted the school's placement service, along with the denomination of my home church. I sent out my résumé and waited for the phone to ring. I prayed that God would give me the wisdom to discern which church would be the right one for me. I guess I expected a bidding war. After several months of waiting the only church that expressed serious interest in me was a congregation of forty-nine people located in a small town in central Illinois. There was no stately building. We met in a storefront in the center of town. There wasn't even a bathroom in the church. The regulars knew to use the bathroom at home before they came. We sent visitors to the neighbor next door who owned the building. I was the only member of the church staff. It was a wonderful experience but it was not the church of my dreams. There were many days when I wondered why God had not called me to a larger place.

AMBITION, OPPORTUNITY AND GOD'S CALL

There is a place for ambition in the Christian life. Ambition is simply a mode of desire and desire is normal. "Desire is primal: to be human is to want," observes Jen Pollock Michel.[5] Michel admits that our desires can sometimes go wrong. But the gospel promises not only to forgive our sin but also to renew our desires. Desire is not itself bad. Much of what we desire is good. Some that is bad can be changed. When ambition fuels our efforts on the athletic field, in business and even in the arts, it can energize us and expand the scope of our success. Ambition also has a place in our spiritual life. We are told to "desire the greater gifts" (1 Cor 12:31). Anyone who sets their heart on church office "desires a noble task" (1 Tim 3:1).

It was ambition that motivated James and John to ask for the honor of sitting at the Lord's right and left hand in glory. "You don't know what you are asking," Jesus said. "Can you drink the

cup I drink or be baptized with the baptism I am baptized with?"
(Mk 10:38). This sounds more like a criticism of their naiveté
than a condemnation of their ambition. "Be careful what you
wish for," Jesus seems to say. "You just might get it." Their kind
of aspiration comes with a price. It is not the cost of attaining a
higher seat but the nature of the calling itself. Jesus warns that
there is a cup of suffering waiting for the one who will occupy
the positions they hope to fill.

Yet ambition, even when it is combined with ability, is not the
only thing that determines whether we achieve our aim. Pursuing rest often means that we must be at peace with the calling
assigned to us by God. This is a matter of divine sovereignty.
Jesus affirms that James and John will drink the cup, but the
place of honor they each desire is not theirs to choose. It is not
even his to offer. Those seats come by divine appointment from
the Father. If the Father has determined that they should go to
someone else, not even Jesus can grant them their wish. This is
a hard saying for those who have been told that they can accomplish anything as long as they try hard enough and believe
in themselves.

We can aspire to anything but we cannot do just anything.
We do not all have the same abilities. Even among those of us
who have ability, we do not all have the same opportunity or
calling. God plays a role. He has "arranged the parts in the body,
every one of them, just as he wanted them to be" (1 Cor 12:18).
This seems to be as true of external circumstances as it is of our
abilities. According to 1 Corinthians 7:17, our circumstances
have been "assigned" to us by God. There are some things we can
change. The single person may choose to marry. The slave in
Paul's day could sometimes gain his freedom (1 Cor 7:21). We
can choose a different career or move to a new location. But it

is not all up to us. My proposal of marriage may be rejected. The slave did not always have an opportunity to obtain freedom.

So how do we distinguish between a circumstance we can change and one that has been "assigned" by God? Some situations are defined for us by Scripture. Now that I am married, whether I remain faithful to my wife or find a new partner is not up for question—I am bound by moral obligation. Other circumstances are determined by a combination of opportunity and initiative. We may have the freedom to change, but to do so we must be given the opportunity and actually choose to act. What does rest look like for those who have been assigned a circumstance by God? It looks like the sentiment expressed in a prayer attributed to theologian Reinhold Niebuhr:

> God, give me grace to accept with serenity
> the things that cannot be changed,
> Courage to change the things
> which should be changed,
> and the Wisdom to distinguish
> the one from the other.

AMBITION'S EVIL COMPANIONS

When James and John approached Jesus and asked to be assigned a place of honor in his kingdom, the other disciples were outraged. This was not because they thought the request lacked humility but because they believed they deserved the honor as much or more than James and John. There was great irony in the timing of this dispute, which came on the heels of Jesus' announcement that he was going to Jerusalem to be betrayed, condemned and executed. The true nature of the disciples' spiritual ambition was exposed when Jesus compared it to that of the rulers of the Gentiles who "lord it over them" and "exercise authority" (Mt 20:25). What Jesus condemns in this dispute goes beyond legitimate ambition. It is the desire to dominate. Jesus' disciples wanted to do more than surpass one another in their devotion. They were angling for positions of superiority and privilege.

This was not the first time the subject had come up. According to Matthew 18:1, the disciples had already come to Jesus and asked, "Who is the greatest in the kingdom of heaven?" By itself the question was neutral enough to apply to anyone. The disciples might have been thinking of the Old Testament patriarchs or those who would come after them. However, Jesus' reply indicates that their list of candidates was much shorter. The true force of the question was, "Which one of us is the greatest in the kingdom of heaven?" It reflects a spirit of competition and comparison. The disciples raised the question again at the Last Supper (Lk 22:24). The tone of their argument reflected an underlying discontent with the current order; some felt they were not being given the recognition they deserved. If their dispute was prompted by Jesus' announcement that he was about to be betrayed, then the question of comparative greatness was also raised in an atmosphere of suspicion and denial.

The trouble with ambition can often be traced to its companions. Ambition likes to keep company with pride and envy. Both these sins were at work in the dispute among the disciples. It was pride that motivated each to nominate himself as the most likely candidate to be regarded as greatest. Envy made them overly sensitive to signs of regard shown to the others. Pride has a particular affinity with envy. Pride is happiest when it provokes envy in others. Envy is pride's cry of affront when it feels that it has been bested. It is this sense of injury that differentiates envy from simple desire or the nobler longing of aspiration. Simple desire often has a positive effect, motivating us to seek that which we desire. Aspiration provides the sustained energy needed to make the ascent to a lofty goal. Envy has the opposite effect. Envy angers but does not energize. When it sees that others possess what it does not, envy feels cheated. It would rather deprive them of what they have attained than seek what it lacks. This is because envy is insecure. It does not believe that possession is really possible.

Envy is explicitly linked with "selfish ambition" in James 3:14. This form of ambition is a collective sin as much as it is a sin of the individual. It speaks of an ambition born of rivalry. On an individual level sinful ambition is self-seeking, attempting to get the advantage over others. Within the community it expresses itself in factions or partisanship. Across different communities it is the spirit that is driven to increase market share at the expense of others.

Pride and envy find it all too easy to influence ambition because ambition is particularly inclined toward competition. It is competition that often impels us to put ourselves forward over another person. Competition is more interested in seeking its own interests than in seeking the interests of others. "There is no denying that competitiveness is part of the life both of an individual and a community, or that, within limits, it is a useful and necessary part," Wendell Berry observes. "But it is equally obvious that no individual can lead a good or a satisfying life under the rule of competition, and that no community can succeed except by limiting somehow the competitiveness of its members. One cannot maintain one's 'competitive edge' if one helps other people."[6]

The pressure to surpass and to be superior to others that

springs from ambition is especially damaging in the spiritual realm. Spiritual ambition causes our interests to contract rather than expand. As a result we focus more on ourselves than we do on others. If we do have regard for others, it is by way of comparison. The angle of vision that spiritual ambition affords is a desperate glance over the shoulder to see if someone is gaining on us. Jesus does allow ambition in the kingdom, but it is of a very different kind. Kingdom ambition is directed toward advancing others instead of surpassing them. The one who is great in Christ's kingdom of rest is not a master but a servant. The only way to compete successfully in this race is to make sure that someone else wins it.

SPIRITUAL CAPITALISM

This may be unsettling to us, steeped as we are in free market thinking. We live in a culture that equates a free market with personal freedom. In a free market society competition is a virtue rather than a vice. It is the key to the success. It is the dynamic that makes the best life possible for a society's residents. Free market thinking believes that people, ideas and goods all improve when they compete against one another. The cream rises to the top. The rest will eventually fall in line with the winners or fail altogether. There is a kind of Darwinism implied in such a philosophy, with its conviction that the battleground of the marketplace enables those who participate to adapt and improve. It is an evolutionary model, willing to trust in survival of the fittest.

In the North American church, free market thinking is blended with spiritual individualism. William Dyrness points out that American culture emphasizes personal growth in a way that defines goodness primarily in terms of what is deemed beneficial for the individual: "The result is that we treat both other people and society at large as opportunities for our individual growth."[7] In such a culture, the value of a thing is determined by its ability to further our own personal development and satisfaction. Not only is this approach inimical to the development of community, it lends itself to narcissistic consumerism. "A major problem with a preoccupation with my individual development is that it provides no intrinsic value 'for you,' except as an environment for my growth," Dyrness observes.[8]

Because we have been taught to relate to the world around us as individualistic consumers, we tend to view personal relationships and the larger community around us as existing for our sake and as replaceable. Everyone and everything becomes a commodity. When this mentality is absorbed by the church, it produces an unhealthy amalgam of spiritual narcissism mixed with religious capitalism. This mentality affects the way we relate to the church. Skye Jethani observes that the cultural shift from manufacturing goods to manufacturing brands has transformed North American Christianity from a faith of substance to a faith of style and perception. "Two generations ago when denominational loyalty was high, a church was chosen primarily based on the doctrinal beliefs it espoused," Jethani explains. "Today, the music style used in worship is the issue of paramount importance when choosing a church."[9]

This blending of spiritual narcissism with religious capitalism also affects the way churches view their mission and their members. Mission is confused with marketing. Souls turn into prospects. Members are treated like distributors whose job is to promote the corporate brand through multilevel marketing. But the brand is not the gospel. The brand is the church itself and often the pastor. For a handful of megachurches the pastor's brand is big business with the potential to generate millions of dollars in income. Churches franchise themselves based on a pastor's celebrity status and the church's corporate style. Disagreements about who owns the rights to the pastor's books and sermons have generated headlines and lawsuits.[10]

Author and filmmaker Jean Kilbourne notes how profoundly our thinking and values have been shaped by the culture of marketing: "We are surrounded by hundreds, thousands of messages every day that link our deepest emotions to products that objectify people and trivialize our most heartfelt moments and relationships. Every emotion is used to sell us something."[11] Marketplace culture debases the way we think about ourselves and the world around us. Instead of seeing ourselves as living eternal souls who have been created in the image of God and as stewards of the created world, we come to understand ourselves primarily as customers. "It leads inevitably to narcissism and solipsism," Kilbourne warns. "It becomes difficult to imagine a way of relating that isn't objectifying and exploitive."[12]

Advertisers seek to do more than get the word out about their product. Contemporary marketing strategies pour billions of dollars into research and image management in an effort to shape the desires of their customers. On the surface it might appear that this is exactly what the church should do. After all, aren't we trying to make the world aware of its need for Jesus Christ? But the trouble with the Jesus brand is that the gospel is fundamentally incompatible with a marketplace culture. The basic rule of the marketplace is that the customer is king. The message of the gospel is antithetical to such thinking because the rule of the gospel is that Christ is king. Jesus Christ did not come merely to improve our lives but to take possession of them. He has no product to peddle and will not place himself on the market.

The branded church turns itself into a commodity when it puts itself on the market. In 2 Corinthians 2:17 Paul contrasts his ministry with those of others who acted like retailers in the marketplace: "Unlike so many, we do not peddle the word of God for profit. On the contrary, in Christ we speak before God with sincerity, like men sent from God." The analogy Paul employs to describe his philosophy of ministry points to a metaphor for understanding the mission of the church that is both sounder and more theologically accurate than any we can borrow from the marketplace. The church's point of comparison for what it does is not the retailer but the prophet. While both have something to communicate, their frame of reference is radically different. Since the retailer is ultimately answerable to the consumer, his or her primary objective is to please the consumer. If the consumer does not buy, the retailer is finished. But the prophet is answerable only to God. It is true that both the church and the retailer need to be deeply interested in those they hope to reach. But the church's interest is priestly in nature. It is an interest that is primarily concerned with the care of souls rather than the consumption of a product. The prophet who places himself on the market is a false prophet. The church that places itself on the market is a prostitute.

BIBLICAL AMBITION

The strange values of Christ's kingdom turn our aspirations on their head. There is a place for ambition but it is an ambition that moves in the opposite direction of the world at large. Instead of aspiring to be great, we are to "become like little children," Jesus says (Mt 18:3). We need to resist the temptation to view Jesus' statement through modern eyes. We think of children as innocent, simple and mostly cute. If we are not careful, we will conclude that Jesus is asking us to embrace a personal style. But Jesus was making a point about humility. Although children were valued in Jesus' day, they had no real status in society. According to Jesus the trajectory of greatness in the kingdom moves in a direction opposite to that of the disciples' thinking. They were aiming toward prominence. Jesus pointed them toward insignificance. The compass he provided located the true north of ambition in a direction that looked to them more like downward mobility than real aspiration.

In other statements Jesus fleshed out some of the implications of this. He warned his disciples away from honorific titles and special treatment implying that they occupied a higher status than others in the community of faith. Instead of the honored teacher, who was called "master" and "father," Jesus set before his disciples the analogy of the household slave. The kind of ambition he urged on his disciples was an ambition to serve more than to be served and to give way to others instead of claiming the most important place for themselves.

> If the primary aim of our ambition is to be noticed, we ought to recall that we live within sight of the one who sees the sparrow fall to the ground.

If the primary aim of our ambition is to be noticed, we ought to recall that we live within sight of the one who sees the sparrow fall to the ground. If our goal is to make a name for ourselves, we should know that our names are written in the Lamb's book of life. If we hope to leave our mark on this world, we ought to rejoice that Jesus Christ has placed his mark on us. We have been sealed by the promised Holy Spirit, who has been put within our hearts as a deposit guaranteeing what is to come. If we aspire to power and wealth, we should know that we have been promised "a rich welcome into the eternal kingdom of our Lord and Savior Jesus Christ" (2 Pet 1:11). We may not be rich ourselves, but we are Christ's rich inheritance. We may not be influential now, but we are part of a kingdom of priests who will one day reign on the earth. If we hoped to find a place at the table, we will not be disappointed. Our seat is reserved at the wedding supper of the Lamb. If it is all for love, Jesus Christ showed us the full extent of his love when he knelt and washed the disciples' feet.

None of these things comes about by our own effort. If we come to them, it is because we have gained entrance by way of gracious invitation rather than by ambition. If they come to us, it is because we have received them as a gift. They are ours by right but not by force of will. They are bestowed on us the way a family name and its inheritance are granted to a child who has done nothing to earn them. They are our birthright as children of God and citizens in Christ's kingdom.

The apostle Paul later summarized Jesus' teaching about ambition by pointing to Christ's own example as a model when he urged believers to "do nothing out of selfish ambition or vain conceit, but in humility consider others better than yourselves. Each of you should look not only to your own interests, but also to the interests of others" (Phil 2:3-4). The ambition of the kingdom is ambition exercised on behalf of others. It inclines us to put others forward before ourselves. It means that we will be more eager to recognize the accomplishments of others than to make certain our own achievements are acknowledged. It is not an attitude of self-neglect, but it is one of self-denial. In Christ's kingdom the highest honor is to be identified with the king, "who, being in very nature God, did not consider equality with God something to be grasped, but

made himself nothing, taking the very nature of a servant,
being made in human likeness. And being found in appearance
as a man, he humbled himself and became obedient to death—
even death on a cross!" (Phil 2:6-8).

The kind of ambition the apostle sets before us is more ordinary than we might expect. Instead of calling us to radical
poverty, epic adventure or rock star celebrity, the apostle out-
lines an agenda that sounds more like the kind of workaday
lives most of us ordinarily lead: "Make it your ambition to lead
a quiet life, to mind your own business and to work with your
hands, just as we told you, so that your daily life may win the
respect of outsiders and so that you will not be dependent on
anybody" (1 Thess 4:11-12). Is pursuing rest the same thing as
living a quiet life? It depends on what "quiet" means. If we
think this means we should idle away our days in some bucolic
setting completely unnoticed by others, then we have a problem.
Most of us live in contexts where that kind of quiet is hard to
come by. A quiet life does not necessarily mean we live in a
quiet neighborhood or fade into the background and become
invisible. One of the aims of living the life that Paul describes
is so that we "may win the respect of outsiders." Quiet in this
context means to live responsibly. Attend to the calling that
God has assigned you. Do not meddle or take advantage of
others. Work as God enables you so that you can meet your
own needs and have something left over to provide for those
who cannot provide for themselves.

Very few of us are called to be famous for God. Most of us
work at our jobs and serve in our churches in relative obscurity.
We are noticed only by a handful of family, friends and
neighbors. If our hearts sink at such a prospect, it can only be
because we have forgotten the burden that comes with self-

oriented ambition. The burden of ambition is the strain of seeking approval. It is the taxing effort to earn the envy of others, many of whom are in competition with us. It is the weight of self-imposed anxiety over the recognition we believe is due us. The burden of ambition is the back-breaking labor required to maintain our place on the record board and defend it against all comers. It is the grief we feel when someone else matches or surpasses our achievement. It is the strain that comes from climbing the ladder combined with the fear of a rapid and unexpected descent. The burden of ambition is the impossible expectation we place on ourselves to be the smartest, funniest, most skilled, most liked or even the most holy person in the room. Self-oriented ambition is not a gift from the Father of lights. It is a bad legacy from the father of lies. We are better off without it.

QUESTIONS FOR REFLECTION

1. Does ambition have a place in the Christian life? If so, how do we distinguish between legitimate and illegitimate ambition? Does ambition always lead to competition? How is envy related to pride? Is competition ever good in the church?

2. What is spiritual capitalism? What does it look like in the church? What does it look like in spiritual life? What are the drawbacks? Are there any benefits? How does marketplace culture shape the way we think about ourselves and the people around us? What happens when this kind of thinking invades the church?

3. What does healthy spiritual ambition look like? How does it differ from selfish ambition? How do we acquire it?

4. How do you feel when others succeed? What are you most ambitious for? How can you test your own ambitions? How can you purify your ambition?

5. In what sense is ambition a burden? What is the antidote?

WORSHIP
as REST

When I was a pastor worship was my job. All the effort of my workweek came to a climax on Sunday morning as the congregation gathered in the church's sanctuary. In the early years I led the musical portion of the service in addition to preaching. All this really meant was that I selected the songs and stood at the podium waving my hands in a vague approximation of the beat. The music was made up mostly of hymns. Usually they were ones that I already knew and that had something to do with the message. I tried to be thoughtful in my selection (although I was somewhat hindered in this by my inability to read music). I was also a little selfish. I tended to pick the songs I liked and avoid those I didn't. Occasionally we sang choruses that I had learned during my days as a Jesus Freak, while I accompanied the congregation on a guitar. The fact that I only knew five chords severely limited my repertoire.

In those days the experience of worship was almost always

meaningful to me. It was hard to understand why everyone didn't see congregational worship as the high point of their week. When I left the pastorate and took my place on the other side of the pulpit something changed. At first I was relieved. "Just think; none of this depends on me," I told my wife one Sunday as the service began. But it didn't take long for me to grow uncomfortable. My new role as a worship attender instead of the worship leader was disorienting. The view seemed all wrong from where I was seated. Instead of seeing the faces of the congregation, all I could see were the backs of people's heads. I no longer enjoyed the freedom of the platform. I felt restless, hemmed in on all sides by other worshipers. I no longer had a say in what was sung or said.

The experience also felt disturbingly familiar. I recognized the slouch in my posture and the look of polite but detached interest that I knew was on my face. I had seen it many times from the pulpit. I also recognized the worship leader's tone of gentle scolding, embellished with a grace note of condescension. We weren't trying hard enough, especially if we had "only" come to worship. I often felt like a deadbeat employee called on the carpet for neglecting my job. That's when it dawned on me. Something was seriously wrong here.

Worship is active but it isn't work. Worship is an obligation but it is also a gift. Worship is a verb but its most important dimension is passive. God is the focus of worship, but we are its primary beneficiaries. Worship isn't work; it is an act of leisure. We think of leisure as something we do in our off time. Leisure is how we spend our weekends. Boating, hiking, watching television—these are all leisure activities. But there is an older and more venerable sense to the word. "Recreation, entertainment, amusement, play—all this is *not* meant here," theologian Josef

Pieper explains.[1] Leisure in the ancient sense is tied to philosophy
and contemplation. It is an attitude of the mind and a condition
of the soul. Leisure is a mode of silence and a way of appre-
hending reality. It is characterized by receptivity and serenity.[2]

If worship is an act then it is an act of leisure. As such worship
does not have to be functional in order to be legitimate. It does
not need to be practical. It is not necessary for those who
worship to produce some additional benefit for the church in
order for their worship is be acceptable. It is enough for them
simply to worship. Worship is "an activity that is meaningful in
itself."[3] This is hard for us to accept in a value-added world that
believes that production alone gives meaning to our existence.
Those who do not produce something of value do not count.
Coming to church "just to worship" seems unproductive.

WHO IS WORSHIP FOR?

Worshipers do not need to produce something in order for their
worship to be legitimate because worship is productive by its
very nature. James K. A. Smith points out that worship is formative: "Historic Christian worship is fundamentally formative
because it educates our hearts through our bodies (which in turn
renews our mind), and does so in a way that is more universally
accessible (and I would add, more universally effective) than
many of the overly cognitive worship habits we have acquired
in modernity."[4] We speak to God in worship but we are also
talking to ourselves. Our worship is directed at God but we are
the ones who benefit from the experience. Smith explains, "To
say that God is both subject and object is to emphasize that the
triune God is both the audience and the agent of worship: it is
to God and *for* God, and God is active in worship *in* the Word
and sacraments."[5]

Worship is a collective expression of the church's faith. Employing a variety of forms (psalms, hymns, spiritual songs), we express our thanksgiving to God through singing. This worship is aimed at more than one audience. The congregation sings "to God" and "to the Lord" (Eph 5:19; Col 3:16). But worship is also a form of self-talk. Worship is a mode of divine instruction, an articulation of what the church believes. The "act" of listening to what is being sung is as important as the act of singing. Worship also makes us aware of the presence of God. The essence of what is happening when the church comes together for worship is expressed in the scenario described in 1 Corinthians 14:25: "God it is really among you!" This is more than an expression of feeling. It is the essence of what it means to be the church. The church is "a dwelling in which God lives by his Spirit" (Eph 2:22). One of the main functions of congregational worship is to mediate the presence of God to those who are present. The primary means for this is the Word of God.

Worship is not a performance. We are not entertaining God when we worship. Nor is the goal of worship to perform in the practical sense of the word. We are not producing something for God when we worship. Although the language of "service" is sometimes used in connection with worship, our worship does not provide God with anything he lacks. God is blessed by our worship in the sense that he is pleased to accept it. But he does not need our worship. God is not any better off because we worship him. He does not depend on us for anything, not even for his own happiness (Acts 17:24-25). We are on the receiving end in worship as much as we are on the giving end. Indeed, it might be said that we are the only ones who receive in worship, since our worship can contribute nothing to God.

This is a necessary correction for a church culture that has come to view corporate worship through the lens of functionality. In many churches worshipers are valued only if they produce something. Those who come for the sole purpose of worship are treated like spiritual deadbeats. In this philosophy worshipers must provide something useful in order to justify their presence. But worship, as an activity that is "meaningful in itself,"[6] does not have to serve any other purpose and those who come to church expecting to receive something from the experience of worship are not abusing it. Although worship involves activity, there is also a passive dimension that is essential to its nature. True worship requires openness and receptiveness. Even when we are active in worship we receive from God.

Those who say that God is the only one who matters in worship are wrong. Worship is for the church. Congregational worship is designed to benefit the congregation as well as glorify God. Through worship we instruct ourselves and proclaim the gospel to the lost. We find recognition and acceptance as members of the community of faith and the household of God. In worship we also find a context in which to face our sin. We speak to God in worship but God also speaks to us. Corporate worship is an event in which believer and unbeliever alike can experience the real presence of the living God.

ENCOUNTERING GOD IN WORSHIP

Corporate worship is sometimes described as the "first base" of discipleship, a designation suggesting that it is only one of the things the church does and perhaps not even the most important thing. In this analogy the ultimate goal of discipleship is serving others, which is seen as the ultimate expression of devotion to God. But theologian Donald Bloesch warns that worship should not be confused with this kind of service. Nor should it be viewed as an atmosphere that pervades our lives in general. "Worship is not simply an attitude that permeates all things Christians do," Bloesch explains, "but an engagement with the sacred in acts of praise and thanksgiving. Service to our neighbor proceeds from worship, but worship is something much more than service. It involves an encounter with the Holy that brings us interior peace and salvation."[7]

In today's church congregational worship often feels more like a sales conference or a motivational seminar rather than an encounter with the holy God. The primary aim is to provide a comfortable environment. Thomas Long captures the atmosphere when he speaks of the "casual chatty preachers of the relaxed suburban congregation, welcoming people with the perkiness of a TV weathercaster and running through the concerns as if they were the recreational program directions of a cruise ship."[8] Cruise ship spirituality rigorously practices congregational climate control in an attempt to ensure that those who attend will have the best possible experience. From the flight attendant smile of welcome offered by the greeters who stand at the door to the breezy patter and top forty enthusiasm of the worship leader to the coffee house ambience of the church foyer, everything in the order of service and the environment is calculated to make sure it is upbeat and enjoyable.

It is not wrong for the church to be interested in the experience of those who attend. But an overemphasis on atmosphere easily turns into image management. Instead of facilitating a true encounter with God through worship and the Word, the church expends most of its resources trying to create an appealing (and often false) impression of what it means to be a follower of Christ and part of the community of believers. The result is an airbrushed picture of the Christian life that is as false as the Photoshop image of a supermodel in a magazine ad.

There is much in Scripture to suggest that an encounter with God produces a kind of holy fear that is also gratifying. Rudolf Otto notes that such an experience is marked by awe combined with an overpowering sense of majesty that is both active and compelling.[9] He describes it as a sense of "that which is quite beyond the sphere of the usual, the intelligible, and the familiar, which therefore falls quite outside the limits of the 'canny,' and is contrasted with it, filling the mind with blank wonder and astonishment."[10]

Consider Luke's depiction of the congregational experience of the Jerusalem church after the deaths of Ananias and Sapphira. After the couple was struck down by God for lying to the Holy Spirit, "great fear seized the whole church and all who heard about these events. The apostles performed many miraculous signs and wonders among the people. And all the believers used to meet together in Solomon's Colonnade. No one else dared join them, even though they were highly regarded by the people. Nevertheless, more and more men and women believed in the Lord and were added to their number" (Acts 5:11-14). The judgment of Ananias and Sapphira and the manifestation of signs and wonders were not the ultimate reasons for this godly fear. They merely pointed to something else. Or rather they pointed to someone else. They were evidence of the living presence of God in the church.

WORSHIP AND PRESENCE

God's presence is not a function of a particular worship style or a ministry method. It is the church's birthright. The reality of God's presence is the basic assumption of Christian worship.

"Christians worship with a conviction that they are in the presence of God," Eugene Peterson explains. "Worship is an act of attention to the living God who rules, speaks and reveals, creates and redeems, orders and blesses."[11] Peterson's characterization of Christian worship as "an act of attention" is especially helpful because it underscores the role of faith in worship. In worship the church acknowledges that God is already present and active. The church does not create that presence. Even when it experiences the reality of Christ's presence through word and sacrament, these actions are responsive rather than generative. They do not work like magic. We cannot compel the living God to show himself on command. God is not at our beck and call. We enter God's presence through worship because we have been invited.

Yet because worship is relational, there is also a reciprocal dimension to this experience. In Revelation 3:20 we find a surprising inversion in which Christ issues the invitation to fellowship with him from outside the church. Although he is the initiator, he does not barge into the church's presence. Instead he waits until he is granted access. It is easy to see why this passage is a favorite text in evangelism. Yet in its biblical context, this gracious invitation was actually extended to the church. How was it possible for the Laodiceans to exclude Christ from their worship? It was because they approached it without an awareness of their own need (Rev 3:17-19).

> God's presence is not a function of a particular worship style or a ministry method. It is the church's birthright.

In the structure of worship this reciprocal dimension is reflected in the call to worship and the invocation that take place at the beginning of the service. In the call to worship the congregation is reminded of God's often-repeated invitation to have fellowship with him. In the invocation the church acknowledges and accepts God's invitation. With these two moves in the order of worship the church throws open the door of welcome and sets the table for fellowship with Christ. In Christ's invitation to the church of Laodicea, he compares the church's fellowship with him to an intimate meal where one friend engages in close conversation with another.

While the presence of God cannot be manufactured during worship, it may be evoked. When the church's music and art are combined with its great traditions of worship, these have the power to stimulate experiences that offer a glimpse of the divine presence "from a distance."[12] These worship practices do not stir up God's presence. Rather, they provide an analogous experience that makes it easier to attend to the reality of the living God. It is important to distinguish the reality and manifestation of God's presence from the means by which we apprehend it. These experiences are not the actual presence of God but point us to it. The phrase "real presence" is usually confined to discussions about the Lord's Supper. Theological traditions disagree about the degree to which Christ is present in the elements or whether he is present at all. Yet despite these differences, it is possible to posit a more general doctrine of presence with respect to worship. The God who is always present everywhere is uniquely present when the church gathers for worship. Christ promised to be present with the church when it gathered in his name. He is always with the church. The church has also been granted the abiding presence of the Holy Spirit. We are being "built together to become a dwelling in which God lives by his Spirit" (Eph 2:22). Whatever differences we may have about the nature of Christ's presence in the Lord's Supper, all Christians can affirm that God is truly present when the church gathers for worship.

However, even though God is always present with his people, he does not always manifest his presence in a tangible form. The reality of God's presence is primarily a matter of faith. The manifestation of his presence is a matter of experience. The reality of God's presence is not confined to any particular location or occasion. As far as his being is concerned, God is as present in the brothel as he is in the congregation. This is not true of the manifestation of God's presence. In the Scriptures manifestations of God's presence were instances of divine self-revelation. God made himself known to specific individuals on particular occasions. Theologian Geerhardus Vos notes that beginning with the Old Testament patriarchs, most theophanies were confined to definite localities within the borders of the land of promise.[13] God has revealed his presence in visible form and by divine action. However, his primary mode of revelation is by word. "In the past God spoke to our forefathers through the prophets at many times and in various ways," the writer of Hebrews observes, "but in these last days he has spoken to us by his Son, whom he appointed heir of all things, and through whom he made the universe" (Heb 1:1-2). Jesus is the ultimate theophany because he is God in the flesh. It is the Word of God that discloses Jesus to us.

Our experience of God's presence is not confined to the church's worship service. It is not even confined to God himself. Peterson echoes the thinking of Otto when he asserts that the holy is often experienced in that which is not God: "In all cultures and times we have the witness of story, song, and ritual honoring this mysterious divine otherness in things and people who are very much present."[14] However, we need to be careful about identifying these experiences, places and people too closely with the divine presence. They are more like an echo than the true voice. The means by which we apprehend God's presence are the ping of the soul that alerts us to the presence of a greater reality beyond the thing that evokes the experience itself. We must not place so much emphasis on the means that they become a substitute for God. Yet neither should we trivialize them. The means by which we worship are often a barometer of our view of God: "The trivialization of God inevitably leads to the trivialization of worship."[15]

WORSHIP AS THE PURSUIT OF REST

Looking at worship through the theological lens of leisure has caused me to reexamine my experience on both sides of the pulpit. Perhaps I was not as engaged as I thought when I was the one responsible for leading worship. Maybe the only reason I seemed to be more interested was because it was part of my job. I hoped that my planning and preparation would create a particular kind of experience. I needed the congregation's cooperation in order for that to happen. I had preconceived ideas about what true worship should look and sound like. When the service fell short of my expectations I found it easy to be disappointed with the congregation.

Now I think I had it backwards. Worship is not a feast we lay out for God. It is the table on which God spreads his feast for us. Worship is not an exercise in conjuring God for the sake of a congregational event. God's presence is ontological. He is present. The reality of that presence is part of what it

> Worship is not a feast we lay out for God. It is the table on which God spreads his feast for us.

means to be the church. If we are the dwelling place of God by his Spirit, then his presence is essential to our identity whenever we come together. We don't compel God to appear by our words or our actions. He has voluntarily and generously identified himself with us. Although we are more aware of him at some moments than we are at others, it can always be said of the worshiping church, "God is surely in your midst."

The environment of worship is one of the things God uses to draw people to the church. But when we reduce worship to a marketing device it turns worship on its head. Such an approach pushes God to the margin and changes the nature of worship. Martin Marty is right to say, "To give the whole store away to match what this year's market says the unchurched want is to have the people who know least about faith determine most about its expression."[16] The church was designed for worship. Worship was also designed for the church. We do not come together as a church to sell a product. We come to meet with God and be refreshed by his Spirit. When we pursue rest in this area of the Christian life, we reject the burden of guilt that has been laid on us by well-meaning worship leaders who say that we are being selfish when we come to church "just to worship." Although it is possible to be self-centered in worship, the desire to experience the presence of God and glorify him in worship is not selfish.

Looking at worship through the lens of leisure has also helped me come to terms with my restlessness in the pew. It has taught me that the church's worship has value that goes beyond my personal experience. Pursuing rest in the realm of worship means that I must be open to the possibility that God is doing something that goes beyond what is happening to me personally. When I approach worship in a state of rest, I give myself over to whatever God is doing. Worship has value for me even when I do not enjoy it. I would rather enjoy it. But I don't need to enjoy the service for it to be genuine worship.

Stanley Hauerwas talks about the need to develop a Christian vision of the world. He says that being a Christian is more than making certain decisions; "it is a way of attending to the world. It is learning 'to see' the world under the mode of the divine."[17] This angle of vision has helped me lay aside the burden of my own expectations when it comes to the church's worship. When I find worship unsatisfying, I try to train my inner vision to see beyond what I am experiencing. This is usually a matter of talking to myself. When I feel like I don't fit in with what's going on, I tell myself that it does not change the fact that I am a member of the body of Christ. When I am bored with the sermon, I note that it does not have to be interesting in order to be true or beneficial. When I don't like the music, I remind myself that it is part of a greater song that has been taken up by heaven and earth. Sometimes I turn to the Bible's description of heavenly worship in the book of Revelation to refresh my vision and get a sense of what is really going on in the service. There I see that the real trajectory of worship is not from earth to heaven but the other way around. Worship begins in heaven and descends to the church. Down through the centuries the church has looked to this description to find a model for its own worship.

Some Christian traditions have attempted to mirror elements of this heavenly picture in their practice. But the images John provides are more like a visual code than a blueprint. He does not seem to be providing us with a manual for corporate worship, or even a portrait of ideal worship, so much as a series of visual images framed in human language that describe a heavenly reality of which we are already a part. When the church acts out these images in its practice, it acknowledges that it is entering into an act of worship that has been going on since eternity past. Rather than attempting to draw heaven down to earth, the church's worship is a way of acknowledging that we have already taken our place before the heavenly throne. All who are united with Christ are already seated with him in the heavenly realms (Eph 2:6). Eugene Peterson explains, "We must never forget that the pictures of wildly celebrative praise in heaven and catastrophic woes wreaked on earth, the exposure of evil in its hideous blasphemies and the revelation of goodness in its glorious adorations—that all this was made out of the stuff of their daily traffic in scripture, baptism, and eucharist. In this heaven-penetrated, hell-threatened environment they lived their daily lives."[18] Earthly worship is an exercise in sustained attention that requires us to train our vision to see reality as God describes it. When we worship we reorient ourselves to God and to the world around us. Rather than an escape from reality, worship as John describes it is a reality check. It reminds us that God is at the center of all things and that we are part of a great assembly that spans both heaven and earth.

I try to imagine our worship joining with the cry of saints and angels gathered around heaven's throne. When at last I am willing to admit that the root problem is not with the music or the worship leader or the congregation but that it is in me, I remind myself that on this side of heaven the church always worships as a company of sinners. Jesus always welcomes sinners to his table. It is the sick who need the doctor. After all, what is our worship but a reverberation of the glee that all of heaven feels when one sinner repents?

Not long ago a colleague invited me to visit her church. Her church's worship style is liturgical and she thought I would appreciate the change. "I think you would really like it," she said with enthusiasm. "I could tell that it was a good church the first time I attended because I fell asleep during the service!"

To most worshipers this would hardly seem like a recommendation. I don't know of anyone else who would say that the true measure of a good service is that it puts you to sleep. But maybe she is on to something. The biblical institution of the Sabbath in all its forms clearly establishes a theological connection between corporate worship and rest. Rest is worship. But the converse is also true. Worship is a kind of rest.

QUESTIONS FOR REFLECTION

1. Who is worship for? In what sense is it for God? In what sense is it for the church? Does it matter whether we "like" worship? Why or why not? What kind of experience should we expect in congregational worship?

2. Some churches use the worship service to attract visitors. Is there anything wrong with this? Do you think it matters to God?

3. How would it change your approach to worship to view it as an encounter with God? Is an encounter with God that leads to the experience of holy fear the same thing as "getting out of your comfort zone"? What is the difference?

4. How does Eugene Peterson's description of worship as an "act of attention" change your understanding of congregational worship? How does the church experience the presence of God in worship?

5. In light of what you have learned during your reading of this chapter, how should you prepare for congregational worship this week?

REST *and the*
DIGITAL AGE

My grandmother was born before the automobile and the airplane. Horse and buggy were the primary mode of transportation when she was a child. By the time she died, astronauts had walked on the moon. Despite widespread television coverage of the event, my grandmother refused to believe it had actually happened. She remained convinced until the day she died that the government had filmed the whole thing on a back lot in Hollywood.

When first I knew her, my grandmother couldn't have been much older than I am now. Yet by a child's standard she seemed ancient. For one thing, she looked old. She wore old-lady dresses with flowered prints and orthopedic shoes with thick black heels. When she came to stay with us, she looked like someone in a photograph out of a history book.

Her thinking was old too. When grandmother lectured us about manners, her sense of etiquette was attuned to the values of the nineteenth century. Once when I stayed with her, the paperboy came to the door to collect his fee. She was visibly agitated after their conversation. "I hope you won't grow up to be a rude boy like him," she said. "He kept spitting through his teeth!" I nodded in solemn assent, even though I had long envied my best friend's ability to perform this very feat.

But it was her relationship to technology that really persuaded me that my grandmother was ancient. She did not drive. She lived in a small house across the Detroit River in Windsor, Ontario, that smelled as old as she looked and seemed a world away from the suburban brick ranch my parents owned. You could see the Ambassador Bridge from her window. Downtown Detroit was just across the river but her neighborhood felt more like a small town—all wooden houses and large porches. My grandmother didn't have a toaster. She used a dinner fork to cook her toast, holding the bread over the open flame from the burner on her ancient gas stove. Even more astonishing to me was the fact that she had no television, only a radio she tuned to the BBC to listen to the queen's address every Christmas. When I stayed at her house, I amused myself by plinking away on an old upright piano she kept in a spare room. To a child whose notion of modern times was shaped by watching the Jetsons, a visit to my grandmother's felt like stepping back in time.

Now I am the one who must seem ancient, or at least old-fashioned, to my children and my students. I remember a time when you could see movies only at the theater or on television. I used to listen to music on a record player (my children still do but only because vinyl has once again become hip). Advanced technology was an FM radio or a reel-to-reel tape recorder. If I wanted to speak to someone at a distance, I had to use a telephone or send a letter through the mail. I can remember a time when the only person who had anything comparable to a smart-phone was Dick Tracy, and that was only in the comics.

I say all this by way of acknowledgment. There is a risk in taking up the subject of rest in a digital age. Digital natives (those who have never known a world without computers) are tempted to dismiss any criticism of digital culture as little more than the grumbling of those who have trouble keeping up with technological advances. Perhaps there is a measure of truth in this. Jesus' observation is also true when it comes to technology: no one wants new wine after drinking the old (Lk 5:39). We who are comfortable with the technology we already have often say the old is better.

Any critique of digital culture also raises a practical question. Let us suppose that there are problems with digital culture. What can we really do about it? Computer technology is now so pervasive, it is impossible to avoid. Our work, family relation-ships, leisure and even our health are now all linked to digital technology. Even the Amish sell furniture over the Internet. There is no going back to the B.C. (before computers) era.

PURSUING REST IN A DIGITAL AGE

As I write this chapter (and all the others that precede it), my attention is divided. I am listening for the chime that tells me I have a new email waiting. When I am at a loss for words, I find it hard to reflect at length about what I should say next. It is so much easier to click away from the screen and log onto Facebook. Or else I scan my favorite newsfeed and check out the latest headlines. To be honest, it's not news. Not really. It's gossip mostly. Headlines about actors, musicians and late-night talk show hosts. I am not especially interested in their stories. But I keep scrolling, cycling past stories I have read more than once.

Hoping all the while that something new and interesting will appear. I am not addicted. I am distracted.

Computer technology has not destroyed my ability to concentrate. But it has made it harder. It has also made rest harder to find. Digital technology has turned our world into one where we are never alone and are always on the job. Most of us don't think it has any effect on our social and emotional well-being. But the digital world is altering the way we view time and schedule our activities. We use our cellphones to track one another.[1] Wherever we go we are accompanied by the constant murmur of distant friends. Even when we turn off the phone some part of us wonders what we have missed.

Digital culture has also broken down the natural boundaries that used to exist between work and rest. Dr. Kimberly Fisher, a research associate at the Center for Time Use Research at Oxford University, observes, "People don't have as much mental space to relax in a work-free environment. Even if something's not urgent, you're expected to be available to sort it out."[2] The last thing I do before I go to bed at night is check my email. If I have a new message, it's usually about my job. If I wake up in the middle of the night, my first instinct is to lean over the nightstand to check for new messages.

The answer to this problem is obvious. All I need to do in order to pursue rest is to disconnect from the digital world. Not permanently but perhaps for a time. It is simple. But it is not easy. The prospect of being unplugged from the grid makes me nervous. This is more than the fear of losing access to information. It is a sense of being detached. I am not a digital native, yet even I feel uncomfortable when I turn off the technology. I feel isolated, cut off not only from the technology but from the relationships it represents.

The technology is new but the fear is an old one. It is solitude I dread. And digital culture makes solitude easier to avoid. When Jesus saw that the people planned to make him a king by force, he "withdrew again to a mountain by himself" (Jn 6:15). This was not the first time Jesus did this. Solitude was his regular practice. But I do not quit the crowd so easily. Not only do smartphones, texting and social media enable others to intrude on me at any time and in every location, they greatly increase the likelihood that I will invite such interruptions. I can withdraw to the mountain like Jesus, but I am never really alone. Digital culture is the new background noise. It is the multitude I carry in my pocket. Its incessant chirping intrudes on my most intimate moments and serves as a constant reminder of the waiting crowd. Rest is harder to find in a digital culture because technology has dissolved the two fundamental boundaries that are essential to rest: solitude and silence.

SOLITUDE AND SILENCE

Interruptions were a problem before there was digital technology. Jesus was interrupted too. The crowd intruded on his privacy on more than one occasion. The difference between his experience and ours is that the crowd had to make a serious effort in order to interrupt him. Today they can stay where they are and click their way into our presence. Like Jesus we occasionally need to withdraw from the crowd—especially the virtual crowd. One solution is to turn to habits the church practiced long before the computer age was ever envisioned: the ancient disciplines of solitude and silence.

Solitude is a critical component to our overall spiritual health. Dallas Willard describes the benefit of solitude this way: "The normal course of day-to-day human interactions locks us into patterns of feeling, thought, and action that are geared to a world set against God. Nothing but solitude can allow the development of a freedom from the ingrained behaviors that hinder our integration into God's order."[3]

The biblical metaphor for solitude is the wilderness. Moses, David, the prophets, Paul, the disciples and of course Jesus himself all spent time in the wilderness. On the surface, the wilderness seems an unlikely location for rest. After all, the wilderness is not a resort. It is a place of deprivation. While we are in the wilderness we do not have access to our usual conveniences. The wilderness is also a place of disruption. Work must cease and we cannot maintain our ordinary relationships. It is impossible to follow our normal routine there.

This sheds an important light on the experience of rest. We are tempted to think of rest as a kind of indulgence. But in reality the practice of rest often involves a measure of self-denial. Rest requires that we cease our ordinary activities and break away from our daily relationships. When we are at rest we are often unavailable.

When God's people observed the Sabbath in the wilderness, they could not gather manna. Instead the Lord preserved the extra food they had gathered on the previous day. God's people were also forbidden from engaging in their ordinary work and were restricted in their movements. But deprivation is not the ultimate goal of rest. The intention was not for the Israelites to go hungry but to recognize that they were being fed by God. They abstained from their normal occupations in order to occupy themselves with something better. Likewise, when we rest in this way we do not cease from all activity; we abstain from one kind of activity in order to engage in another. We deprive ourselves of our ordinary work for a time in order to engage in a higher calling with a better reward. The benefit we receive by leaving our other pursuits behind is that we are refreshed. The ancient command to observe the Sabbath was both a sign and an invitation to enter into the experience of God, who refreshed himself on the seventh day of creation. The pursuit of rest is really the pursuit of God.

This is the goal when we practice solitude. We deprive ourselves of the companionship of others in order to enjoy better company. We remove ourselves from the presence of a spouse, our children or our friends to seek the companionship of God. Even though God is our constant companion, it is often hard to give him our undivided attention. When we practice solitude we place ourselves in an environment that enables us to focus our attention on him exclusively. The more inaccessible we are, the easier it is to do this. I sometimes go to a cottage near a beach that does not have television reception or Internet access. It is far from my office and I know relatively few people in the community.

> The pursuit of rest is really the pursuit of God.

But it is also three and a half hours away. The steps required to find solitude do not always have to be so elaborate. Radical pursuit does not necessarily demand extreme conditions. We do not need to look for a cave or a deserted island. If we can discipline ourselves to turn off the television, computer and phone, a favorite chair in a comfortable room in our own house will do just as well.

There is a risk that comes with the practice of solitude. I have learned to appreciate solitude through experience, but I do not always enjoy it. At least not at first. Solitude removes me from the companionship of others and places me in the company of

God. The aim is to increase my awareness of God, but I often begin by being more aware of myself. Solitude is a mirror and I do not always like what it shows me. In Scripture solitude is often a place of testing and temptation. It is a context in which we are forced to face our weaknesses and shortcomings. It is the place where Satan confronts us with our sin.

Fortunately, solitude is also a sanctuary. Practicing solitude creates a kind of relational space that in time allows God's presence to come to the forefront. Solitude provides distance from our circumstances so we can see how his presence extends to the larger landscape of our lives. The attention required by our relationships and our work frequently obscures this view, so that we suffer from the spiritual equivalent of nearsightedness. We see the problems and the people clearly but we do not see God moving in the midst. Solitude allows a different kind of vision to develop. Like Jacob awakening from sleep, we look at the larger context of our lives and say, "Surely the LORD is in this place, and I was not aware of it!" (Gen 28:16).

This change of perspective does not come instantly. The amount of time I give to solitude must be substantial enough to allow such an inversion to occur. A few minutes may provide some relief but it will not change my point of view. Few people, however, can bear sustained exposure to solitude without practice. It may be better to begin incrementally by seeking a place of solitude for a few minutes every day and gradually expand the amount of time you spend there. Combine the experience of solitude with other disciplines that are suited to the pursuit of rest and can strengthen your sensitivity to God's presence. Fasting, meditation, prayer and even sleep are good choices. Dallas Willard gives solitude first place among the disciplines of abstinence: "Of all the disciplines of abstinence, solitude is generally the most fundamental in the beginning of the spiritual life, and it must be returned to again and again as that life develops."[4] But solitude is not our normal state. In prison solitude is a form of punishment. Human beings were designed for companionship. This is why solitude is a category of rest. It involves the deliberate decision to refrain from human company for a time. It is a discipline, not a lifestyle.

SOLITUDE'S NATURAL COMPANION

Silence is solitude's natural companion and, like solitude, it is not our natural state of being. We are never really in a place of absolute silence. Even in a truly soundproof room, we can still hear the sound of our own breathing or the beating of our heart. We may relocate ourselves to a "quiet" place, but we will inevitably choose to listen to some sounds and block out others. This in essence is what happens when we engage in the discipline of silence. We are not really listening to silence at all but practicing the art of intentional listening. We filter out some sounds and give preference to others. Silence is an exercise in selective rest, choosing to abstain as much as possible from certain sounds. When we pursue rest through silence, we discover how much we use sound to shield ourselves both from our own thoughts and even from God himself. By engaging in silence, we turn away from the constant chatter of the digital world in order to grasp the mysterious ways God speaks to us when we turn our attention to him. Most of the time he speaks to us through his Word. But when we are in solitude and silence we learn to be sensitive to some of the other ways God directs us. Sometimes it is by impressions that are felt deep within the soul. At other times distance from our ordinary circumstances opens our eyes to the patterns in our life that are the marks of his hand.

There are other "sounds" that we must contend with while in silence. These are not audible noises but internal voices that demand our attention. Sometimes it is the sound of our conscience, which either accuses or excuses us. More often it is the white noise of our random thoughts. When we enter into silence the experience is initially infused with the momentum of all that preceded it. Even though we have entered a state of rest, our thoughts are still in motion. They are not orderly. Our inner dialogue sounds like the babble of confusion. As soon as we silence one, another speaks up. It takes time to settle the crowd. If you want to pursue rest through silence, you will need to give yourself enough time to allow this inner noise to settle.

The discipline of silence can also involve the practice of refraining from speech. The Bible has many warnings about the dangers of talking too much: "When words are many, sin is not absent, but he who holds his tongue is wise" (Prov 10:19; see also Eccles 5:3). Of all the members of the body, the tongue seems to be especially vulnerable to the impulses of the sinful nature. Our words can be a wall that deflects the conversation of others and keeps us from listening or understanding. This mode of silence is unnerving because it is essentially passive. When we are truly silent, we are receptive and vulnerable. We are listening.

Most of what passes for listening today is not listening at all. It is merely a pause between sentences. We are busy formulating our next statement while the other person goes on talking. Genuine silence is different. When we are silent we yield the floor. Someone else takes control of the conversation. The intentional practice of silence is also the pursuit of rest because it teaches us to depend on God to look out for our interests. When we practice silence, we surrender. We give up the fight for control.

I have to admit that being silent is not easy for me. I am a verbal processer and a habitual interrupter. When there is a gap in the conversation, I feel compelled to fill the void. In meetings I grow anxious when someone else is speaking while I wait to share my opinion. Many times I don't wait. I interject my point before the other is finished in an effort to take control of the conversation. I frequently overparticipate and feel remorse afterward. The disciplines of solitude and silence provide rest not only from the anxiety of silence but from myself. These disciplines operate like the exercises involved in physical therapy—small but repeated actions that target a specific set of muscles. They aren't exactly strenuous, but they aren't easy either. The experience of silence teaches me that it is possible to engage in focused listening. I learn to refrain from speaking for extended periods of time.

Another way to practice the discipline of silence is to engage in a modified fast from speech. Try to spend a day speaking only when someone else speaks first. Do not initiate conversation and keep your responses to a minimum. Let others have the last word. Combine this with a complete fast from email and social media. You will find a new sense of relief and freedom. The world that was created when God spoke it into being does not depend on your words for its continued existence. Practicing a modified fast from speech shows me that my contribution to the conversation is not always necessary. Other better ideas may surface if I let someone else have the last word. Silence comes as a relief.

STRATEGIC UNPRODUCTIVITY

We tolerate the perpetual background noise generated by the digital world because we think it makes us more productive. But if we want to pursue rest, we must learn how to be unproductive. Rest demands that we be in a state of leisure. Josef Pieper defines "leisure" as a mental and spiritual attitude that requires non-activity and silence. Because leisure is a form of waiting, there must be an element of passivity in it. Those who are at leisure are not trying to be productive. They let things happen: "Leisure is not the attitude of mind of those who actively intervene, but of those who are open to everything; not of those who grab and grab hold, but of those who leave the reins loose and who are free and easy themselves— almost like a man falling asleep, for one can only fall asleep by 'letting oneself go.'"[5] Solitude and silence are not merely disciplines; they are exercises in trust. Those who practice solitude and silence rest in God's control. He is fully capable of running the world without our help.

Solitude and silence are countermeasures for a world that tries to persuade us that our worth is measured by our usefulness. These experiences remind us that we have intrinsic value to God. We do not have to produce to be loved and accepted by him. Indeed, our capacity to produce and the things that are produced by us are all gifts of grace. According to John 15:4, they are the result of abiding in Christ. To abide is to stay in place. It is what the Spirit did when he came down from heaven in the form of a dove at Jesus' baptism. Abiding is a form of rest. We produce fruit but we do not manufacture it. When we engage in solitude and silence we practice the art of abiding.

> Solitude and silence are counter-measures for a world that tries to persuade us that our worth is measured by our usefulness.

Should we be afraid of technology? Perhaps not. Yet neither should the church blindly adopt every new technology that develops without asking serious questions about its implications. Technology is not the enemy of the church. But the church does have an enemy who will not hesitate to use every wile against us. If he can use what God has created to tempt us to sin, it is certain that he can turn our own devices against us.

QUESTIONS FOR REFLECTION

1. How has technology helped your spiritual life? Where has it been a hindrance? Are some areas more affected than others? If so, which areas have been affected most? Why do you think this is?

2. Do you find it hard to "unplug" from the digital world? Is one form of media more difficult to abstain from than another?

3. In what ways has digital culture made it difficult for you to experience rest? Is this a problem created by the technology or something else? Are there any simple steps you can take to address this problem?

4. What do solitude and silence look like in your life? What steps can you take to practice these disciplines?

REST *and* the FUTURE

When I was growing up, Labor Day was the last melancholy holiday of summer. It was the day that signaled the passing of summer vacation and the start of a new school year. With the long sunny days that once stretched endlessly before me finally spent, the arrival of Labor Day meant that my freedom and indolence had come to an end. The reminder was always unwelcome, as uncomfortable as the stiff pants my mother purchased for me during our annual back-to-school pilgrimage to Montgomery Ward.

Even now when Labor Day arrives the scent of grill smoke is mixed with a tinge of melancholy. After all these years I hate to watch summer loosen its grip and give way to the cooler and busier days of fall. Soon the days will grow dark early and the air will turn chill. "Man is like a breath," the Psalmist says; "his days are like a fleeting shadow" (Ps 144:4). The fading days of summer remind me of my own swift passage through the years.

I am getting older and there is nothing I can do about it: "Old age, with all its train and retinue of weakness and infirmities, will come."[1]

Television commercials give the impression that the only difference between youth and old age is a stylish wisp of gray hair. They imply that I can still function like a twenty-year-old, with a little help from certain medications, minor cosmetic surgery and a good financial planner. They exploit the discomfort I feel about the changes taking place in my life and my body. They suggest that these changes can be reversed if I purchase their products. But experience tells me differently. I can feel my strength ebbing as I grow older. My capacity for work is changing. My friends and family are passing away. Age is a chill wind that portends not only the end of life's summer but the end of all things.

FEAR OF THE FUTURE

The days go faster as I grow older. I find myself regretting that I have been in such a hurry to meet them. Albert Einstein is reported to have said, "I never think of the future; it comes soon enough." The same cannot be said of me. I think about the future constantly. Most of my youth was spent in school, preparing for the future. When I was a pastor much of my energy was devoted to implementing my "vision" for the church's future. As a professor in a Bible college, I spend my days training the next generation of church leaders. The future is never very far from my view.

But if the future is a place where I meet my expectations and desires, it is also the point where the present ends. I look forward to vacation. But as soon as it arrives I start calculating the number of days left until it is over. The sharp pleasure I feel when the party begins is blunted by the clock that reminds me it will also come to an end. The future is not a destination. It is a current that carries the happy present downstream and bears it away. Once it is past an experience cannot be relived. It can be recalled only as a memory.

I have also learned that the future is not always an improvement on the present. My health can decline. My dreams may dissolve into regret. What lies ahead can turn out to be something I dread. Jesus shuddered as he considered the looming shadow of the cross in Gethsemane. It is

> If the future is a place where I meet my expectations and desires, it is also the point where the present ends.

hard to know how to deal with the anxiety that comes hand in hand with the future. I cannot plan for it. I do not seem to be able to overcome it by sheer force of will. "You do not get over being afraid by trying not to be afraid," Stanley Hauerwas warns. "Indeed we usually find that attempts to will our way out of being afraid only make us more fearful."[2] According to Hauerwas the only real remedy is to acquire a different kind of fear. The biblical word for this sort of fear is "reverence" or "awe." Jesus spoke of this kind of healthy fear when he told his disciples not to fear those who can kill the body but to "fear him who, after the killing of the body, has power to throw you into hell" (Lk 12:5).

A few years ago I sat on a stiff-backed chair in my doctor's office, wondering why they had painted the walls such an ugly color. After several minutes the doctor entered with a clipboard. He made small talk and in a pleasant voice began to go over some test results. The medical details were mostly beyond me. I listened politely, expecting him to finish and send me on my way.

Instead he took out a pencil and pointed to an image with gray spots. In the same pleasant tone he had used for small talk he said, "You have cancer here and here."

Few words have the power to chill the soul like the word *cancer*. Hearing my doctor's words was profoundly disorienting, more like an out-of-body experience than a clinical diagnosis. I felt like I had been transported to another world, perhaps even another dimension. Once the formula was pronounced over me, like some strange and terrifying sacrament uttered by a priest, I feared I would never be the same again.

I suppose in a way I was right. I left the doctor's office that day with a number to call to schedule surgery and assurances that this would likely take care of the problem. After three years he seems to be right. But something inside me has changed. There is an uncertainty that was not there before. My future is tinged with fear. A nagging worry repeatedly comes to mind: If this has happened to me, how do I know something worse is not going to come next?

Fear is the emotion we feel when we are confronted with something that is greater than us and over which we have no control. When Jesus describes a different kind of fear, he points us to God's loving intent. The God who has power over the body is also the one who has numbered the hairs of our head. He does not forget the sparrow when it is sold for small change. As comforting as this is, it is also somewhat unsettling. Because Jesus' words about the body clearly imply that our enemies might well have their way. When Jesus is finished with his saying, the power of our enemies is still intact. God does not sweep them away with a word. My enemies can still kill me. My cancer could come back. The boss could fire me. Any number of unwelcome things could happen to me and there is nothing I can do to stop it. My future is not at all certain.

This is indeed a cause for wonder. God whose power is greater than my enemies does not always protect me from my enemies. This is no contradiction. Neither is it an abdication of his protection. God still sees. He has numbered my days (Ps 39:4). The worst that my enemies can do does not remove me from God's sight or place me beyond the bounds of his loving care. Yet my devotion to this powerful and loving God might just cost me my life.

The same holds true of our experience in the natural world. The sweeping promises of Psalm 91 assure us that those who take refuge in the most high God come under his protection:

> You will not fear the terror of night,
>   nor the arrow that flies by day,
> nor the pestilence that stalks in the darkness,
>   nor the plague that destroys at midday.
> A thousand may fall at your side,
>   ten thousand at your right hand,
>   but it will not come near you. (Ps 91:5-7)

We are comforted by these words. Yet even as we read them, we can't help recalling many who have succumbed to pestilence despite the psalmist's assurances. I know of many Christians who believed the psalmist's promise and died of cancer anyway. The future is a mixed blessing, even for those who are under God's protection. The psalm is a comfort but it does not promise immunity from the collateral damage of sin. Neither is it a guarantee that the future I experience on this side of eternity will turn out to be everything I hope. I might actually find the psalmist's assurances to be a stumbling block if I did not keep

in mind that this was the same psalm that Satan used when he
took Jesus to the pinnacle of the temple and urged him to jump:

> "If you are the Son of God," he said, "throw yourself down.
> For it is written:
>
> "'He will command his angels concerning you,
>   and they will lift you up in their hands,
>   so that you will not strike your foot against a stone.'"
>   (Mt 4:5-6)

This was a temptation, urging Jesus to reveal his power. But it
was also a taunt, perhaps alluding to the cornerstone promise of
redemption in Genesis 3:15:

> And I will put enmity
>   between you and the woman,
>   and between your offspring and hers;
> he will crush your head,
>   and you will strike his heel.

Jesus unraveled sin's curse by striking his foot against a stone
that struck back. Satan was defeated precisely because Jesus was
not spared according to the psalmist's promise. "Does God
then forsake just those who serve him best?" C. S. Lewis once
asked. The answer appears to be yes, at least on one occasion.
"When God becomes man, that Man, of all others, is least comforted by God, at his greatest need."[3] Lewis marvels at this
apparent contradiction and ascribes it to mystery. He also
warns us not to draw hasty conclusions about ourselves when
our own prayers are answered: "If we were stronger, we might
be less tenderly treated. If we were braver, we might be sent,
with far less help, to defend far more desperate posts in the
great battle."[4]

We shouldn't draw hasty conclusions about the future either. Which is really just another way of saying that we need to be careful about the conclusions we draw regarding the present. Psalm 91:1 promises, "He who dwells in the shelter of the Most High will rest in the shadow of the Almighty." This is a rest of location rather than one of relaxation. It is a position more than it is an emotional state. To rest in this sense is to abide. Those who belong to God are under his protection, even when the worst happens to them. We can be killed but we cannot be dispossessed. Neither the present nor the future nor any other power associated with them can remove us from the sheltering love of God.

Rest is not the absence of fear; it is the presence of trust. The radical pursuit of rest has not eliminated my fears about the future. It has taught me to counter those fears by referring them to God who has control over all things. He is the Lord of the past as well as the future. He is Lord of the distant past that has shaped my present.

IN BONDAGE TO DECAY

People have speculated for millennia about God's relationship to the things that happen in the world—especially the bad things. To what extent is God responsible? To what extent are we? The question is a serious one. The fact that philosophers and theologians have been unable to agree with one another on the subject does not make it less worthy of our consideration. But it should warn us that a simple answer to these questions is probably beyond our reach. If we lean too far in the direction of divine causality, we strip God of his goodness. If we move too far toward human responsibility, we rob God of his supremacy. If we ignore the question of God altogether and look

to nature alone, we find neither freedom nor comfort. Instead,
we find that nature is a horror rather than a relief. The natural
world is a realm, as David Bentley Hart observes, where life
feeds on life:

> It is as if the entire cosmos were somehow predatory, a
> single great organism nourishing itself upon the death of
> everything to which it gives birth, creating and devouring
> all things with a terrible and impassive majesty. Nature
> squanders us with such magnificent prodigality that it is
> hard not to think that something enduringly hideous and
> abysmal must abide in the depths of life.[5]

The apostle Paul makes a similar observation when he describes creation as being in bondage to decay. Viewed through
the lens of nature alone, the primary trajectory of the future
appears to be one of entropy and death. But the apostle provides
a different angle of vision by revealing that creation was "subjected to frustration . . . in hope" (Rom 8:20). God's ultimate
purpose for the future is liberation. The shape of that future is
the glorious freedom of the children of God. This is a view of
creation that understands the present in light of both the past
and the future.

The legacy of the past is a created world that has been subjected to frustration "not by its own choice, but by the will of the
one who subjected it," that is to say by God himself. This took
place when God pronounced the curse of Genesis 3:17-19. It is
this curse, part of the penalty for Adam's sin, that helps us understand why things so often don't turn out as well as we had
hoped. There is a force at work in the world that stands in op-
position to us. It answers desire with struggle and turns even
God-ordained effort into toil. The curse of sin means that for

the present the best of creation cannot be all it was meant to be. Consequently, the legacy of Adam's sin is one of unfulfilled longing, even when we get what we want.

God consigned creation to futility and decay as a kind of exclamation point, a forceful reminder to all who would come after of the gravity of Adam's sin. But it also introduced a forward momentum into the world. This is an impetus Paul compares to the groaning of someone who is in labor and is eager to give birth (Rom 8:22). What's more, there is embedded in this impetus an implied promise of restoration for Adam's children. As Paul describes it, the eager expectation of creation will be deferred until the full redemption of God's children. Creation will share in redemption but the children come first. Redemption rightfully belongs to them. In this way the futility of the created world functions like a signpost pointing us toward a redemption that has not yet been fully realized.

As a result we now travel a landscape whose features reflect both glory and decay. We also make our way along this path with a kind of dual citizenship. On the one hand we live in a world that has been broken by sin. We are subject to frustration along with the rest of creation. At the same time, by virtue of our union with Christ, we are seated "in the heavenly realms in Christ Jesus" (Eph 2:6). We must deal with the ravages of sin even as we experience the transforming work of the Spirit. The Spirit's work will not be completed on this side of eternity but will culminate in the believer's bodily resurrection. This final transformation is necessary because the future God has in store for us requires that we be remade along with the world in which we live. Like the rest of creation, we are leaning into the future, looking forward to a renewed heaven and earth in which righteousness dwells.

THE FUTURE HAS TWO HORIZONS

This means that our future has two horizons. One is a near horizon and the other a far horizon. It is on the far horizon that we see "the Son of Man sitting at the right hand of the Mighty One and coming on the clouds of heaven" (Mt 26:64). This is the future of the new heavens and the new earth. It is the domain of eschatology. The events that lie on the future's far horizon are beyond our immediate reach. The nearer horizon, on the other hand, is the future of our dreams and plans. This is the domain of short-term goals and what we usually call long-range planning. When we invest our money or save for retirement, we do so for the near future. The near horizon is the realm of action and change. It is the future I worry about. The far horizon is the realm of faith and fulfillment. The events that lie on the horizon of the distant future are certain because they have been promised in Scripture. Those that are part of the near future are less certain. As Proverbs 19:21 observes, "Many are the plans in a man's heart, but it is the LORD's purpose that prevails."

An example from the life of David illustrates the difference between these two horizons. According to 2 Samuel 7, once David was firmly established as king over Israel and settled in his palace, he began to feel guilty over the disparity between his richly appointed palace and the tabernacle of God. David called the prophet Nathan to him and said, "Here I am, living in a palace of cedar, while the ark of God remains in a tent." The prophet did not even wait for David to finish his thought. "Whatever you have in mind, go ahead and do it," the prophet replied, "for the LORD is with you" (2 Sam 7:2-3).

We should not be surprised by the prophet's quick assent. Everything David touched seemed to bear the mark of the God who "had given him rest from all his enemies around him" (2 Sam 7:1). Why shouldn't David be the one to build God a house? His motives seem to have been good. He was intent on honoring God. What's more, David had been singularly blessed by God. What better way to show his gratitude than by building a glorious temple? The idea appeared to be a no-brainer to Nathan. It would have seemed the same to us.

Yet that night the word of the Lord came to the prophet with a question for David: "Are you the one to build me a house to dwell in?" The implied answer was "no." The Lord had never asked for a "house of cedar" (2 Sam 7:5-7). If God had wanted something better, he would have provided it for himself.

Old Testament scholar Robert Alter explains, "Here, the argument God makes is that it is an act of presumption for a mere mortal to build a temple for the unhoused God of Israelite history. But this line of reasoning actually enhances the theological importance of Solomon's temple, for it suggests that God Himself will build a house when He is good and ready, using the human agency He chooses."[6] Instead of permitting David to build a house for him, the Lord promised to "establish a house" for David by giving him a descendent whose dynasty would last forever (2 Sam 7:11). However, David was not entirely off the mark in his desire. There was to be a temple in Israel's future. But it would be constructed in God's own time and by a different builder: "When your days are over and you rest with your fathers, I will raise up your offspring to succeed you, who will come from your own body, and I will establish his kingdom. He is the one who will build a house for my Name, and I will establish the throne of his kingdom forever" (2 Sam 7:12-13).

Was it wrong for David to consider such a plan? Not according to God, who told David that he had done well to have such a desire in his heart. Yet the Lord also made it clear that David was the wrong person for the job he had envisioned. For one thing, the timing was not right. Despite the current peace David was enjoying, his fighting days were not over. The temple was to be built during a time of peace. Furthermore, David's violent past disqualified him from the task. God wanted the temple to be built by a man of peace. Solomon, David's son whose name meant "peaceable," would be the one to execute the project.

Yet David did play an important role. He was the one who purchased the land on which the temple would eventually be built. He gathered materials and contributed from his own personal wealth for its eventual construction. David advised Solomon and had a hand in the design. But overall, his part in the project was restricted by present circumstances, prior choices and God's plan.

Like David, we make plans for the future that are often adjusted by God. We can misread God's intent. Even when we grasp his intent, we do so imperfectly. We may grow frustrated when we attempt to execute our perfect plan only to find that God takes it in a different direction. David is also a reminder that the horizon of the near future is shaped by the past. The future is not a blank page on which we may write anything we please. It is often the point where the past catches up with the present. Yet David's story also shows where the near horizon of the future meets the far horizon. God's promise to David reflected a kind of double vision that held both in view at the same time. The promise on the near horizon focused on Solomon and the temple he would build in Jerusalem. But there was someone else on the far horizon of the distant future. The eternal kingdom described in 2 Samuel 7:13 ultimately belonged to a descendant who would be greater than Solomon. Jesus is the architect and builder of a greater temple through the resurrection.

David's experience is a striking example of the capacity God's grace has to draw all things into its power. Remarkably, God's promised temple was built on a landscape littered with the remains of David's foolish choices and sinful actions. The plot of land on which Solomon's temple would eventually be built was acquired by David after he sinned by numbering the people. God's chosen instrument for constructing the temple is Solomon, the fruit of a marriage that grew out of David's greatest sin.

Christ's kingdom is the point where the past, present and future ultimately converge. This kingdom is like the river of the water of life that flows from the throne of God and the Lamb. It has the power to reverse the damage done by sin's curse (Rev 22:1-3). In the believer's experience the current of Christ's kingdom operates bidirectionally. It flows forward, linking the horizon of the near future with the horizon of the distant future. But it also moves backward, drawing all things into its power. C. S. Lewis suggests that in eternity the redeemed and the damned will share a similar bipolar view: "The good man's past begins to change so that his forgiven sins and remembered sorrows take on the quality of Heaven: the bad man's past already conforms to his badness and is filled only with dreariness."[7] Consequently, when we finally reach the far horizon, we will see that God was at work "in all things ... for the good of those who love him" (Rom 8:28).

> Christ's kingdom flows forward, linking the horizon of the near future with the horizon of the distant future. But it also moves backward, drawing all things into its power.

This perspective will not change the details of our past. The bad things we have done will not suddenly disappear from the timeline of our lives as if they had never existed. Nor will it change the character of the past. That which was bad will not suddenly become good. Evil will not prove to have been something else. Yet the current of God's grace shown to us in Christ will redeem our past. Our view of it will change. More importantly, we will be changed. The debris of the past will prove to have been the stuff of transformation, used by God for our good. This transformation can be viewed only partially from our current vantage point. We experience a foretaste through the Spirit of God, but its full extent remains to be seen. The radical pursuit of rest is a way of looking at the past as much as it is a perspective on the future. By it we learn to surrender the past to God.

AGE IS NOT THE ENEMY

Age is not the enemy. Neither is the passage of time. It is the collateral damage sin has wreaked on the aging process that creates a problem for us. Gilbert Meilaender observes, "Unlike disease, aging is a normal stage of life that seems 'built in.' It makes us more vulnerable to disease but is not itself pathology. No one dies because his hair turns gray, and the diseases often associated with old age can occur even apart from aging."[8] Indeed, in a number of passages the Bible speaks positively about aging. Gray hair, the symbol of age, is "the splendor of the old" (Prov 20:29). This is not a statement about the cosmetic advantages of a "touch of gray," like the images portrayed to us by marketers. Gray hair is emblematic of experience and wisdom. If physical strength is the advantage of youth, wisdom born of experience is the benefit of age. Old age is a crown, not a curse. The second-century church father Irenaeus declared "the glory of God is man fully alive." Scripture would also say that the glory of God is a person fully mature. Age is an asset rather than a liability.

Yet the Bible is also realistic about the challenges that come with aging. Aging is uncomfortable, especially in its final stages. The descent into weakness and eventual death is often marked by an equally painful loss of identity and disintegration of relationships. "To grow old is to lose our acquaintances and lifelong friends to distance, illness, and death," Stanley Hauerwas and Laura Yordy remind us. "As our friends move away or die we lose the confirmation of our own life stories and identities. We are not even sure, as we grow old, that we are still the same people we were."[9]

The experience of age is also no guarantee of wisdom. Left to ourselves, long experience is just as liable to make us prideful and stubborn as it is to make us humble and wise. The humiliations that accompany aging can strip away our pretense so that only humility remains—or they can leave us scarred and bitter. Without the shaping influence of God's Word combined with the mitigating effects of his grace, age is as likely to ravage as it is to bless. "There is no point in imagining old age, especially in its last years, to be easy; nor should we expect that many of us will have a lot of 'golden years,'" warns Maxine Hancock. "From what I have observed, what lies ahead is more like a rock-climbing expedition, straight up a rock face, and then a slipping and sliding down through the shale on the other side to the place of our 'crossing over.'"[10]

This may actually be aging's final gift to us. Age is what ushers us to the threshold of eternity. But it is often the decline that attends us on the last leg of the journey that makes us eager to step across. It is not ordinarily in our nature to welcome death. We cling to life. Our grasp on life is so tenacious that some of us would accept a significantly diminished life before we would yield to the alternative. As Ecclesiastes 9:4 wryly observes, "Anyone who is among the living has hope—even a live dog is better off than a dead lion!"

If there is a hidden grace behind the frailty that accompanies old age, it is the power it has to loosen our grip on this first life and abandon ourselves to a second: "For while we are in this tent, we groan and are burdened, because we do not wish to be unclothed but to be clothed with our heavenly dwelling, so that what is mortal may be swallowed up by life" (2 Cor 5:4). The longing Paul describes in this verse is not a longing for death. It is a longing for life. What's more, it is a longing for embodied life—a desire "to be clothed with our heavenly dwelling" (2 Cor 5:2). This groaning, which may be all too literal at times, is an expression of our desire for a different kind of body, and along with it a different kind of life. This too is a kind of rest. It is resignation in the most positive sense of the word. The biblical word we use to describe it is *hope*.

It is no wonder that we do not welcome old age. The frailty and decline that come with it are not only uncomfortable; they are harbingers of death. It is good to be brought up short and reminded that there is a limit to this life and that another awaits us beyond it. Summer may be over, but the vacation has yet to begin. For those who belong to Jesus Christ, when this life's day is finally spent, there is another, better rest waiting for us.

QUESTIONS FOR REFLECTION

1. When do you think most about the future? How do you think about it? When are you most inclined to worry about the future? In what sense might we say that the future is a mixed blessing?

2. We often struggle to understand God's control of the future. What is the danger of placing all our emphasis on divine causality without taking human responsibility into account? What happens if we place most of our emphasis on human responsibility? What if we rule God out altogether?

3. Is it wrong to plan for the future? Why or why not? How do we discern the difference between responsible planning and presumption? Can you think of a time when your plans did not match God's? How did you know? How did you react when you discovered that God's plan for your life differed from your own?

4. Our future has both a "near horizon" and a "far horizon." What is the difference between these? Which horizon occupies most of our future? Which horizon is the focus of most of our planning? Why is this?

5. What does it mean to leave the future in God's hands? Does this eliminate the need for planning?

FINAL REST

My little dog is dead. A toy Yorkshire terrier named Luigi, he lived to be thirteen—a ripe old age for a dog. Already lame from arthritis and blind in one eye, when Luigi lost the sight of his other eye we knew the time had finally come to put him down.

A friend had given Luigi to us. She loved the dog but felt like she wasn't home enough to keep him. It didn't take long for us to see why. Like the rest of his breed, our little dog had an insatiable appetite for human companionship. This only intensified as he aged. Luigi hated to be alone. It was not enough for him to be in the same room with us; he had to be as close as possible. Preferably on someone's lap.

Although he was happy to spend time with anyone, my wife, Jane, was the real center of Luigi's universe. Whenever she sat on the couch, Luigi was right there with her, his head in her lap and gazing worshipfully into her eyes. As he got older the joy he expressed when she came home bordered on hysteria. This trait endeared him to my wife, whom Luigi had correctly

identified as the true alpha in our little pack. Luigi followed Jane
around when she was at home and, when she was away, sta-
tioned himself near the door to watch for her return. My companionship would do only in an emergency. Jane was the real
love of his life.

This dynamic, as you can imagine, was a recipe for a love
triangle that would be the envy of any soap opera. And my dog
knew he had me at a disadvantage. It is true that I was the one
with the larger brain. But I am less portable and not nearly as
cute. I am more easily distracted, given to alternating fits of
work and television. In the evening when my little dog snuggled
next to my wife, I sometimes caught him watching me out of
the corner of his eye, as if plotting my demise. But as soon as
Jane left the room he would make his way over to my side of the
couch and plop down with a sigh, content as Lazarus when the
angels laid him in the bosom of Abraham.

I never thought of myself as a dog person. I grew up with
cats—disagreeable ones at that. I never really wanted a pet. But
over the years my pup's capacity for canine devotion captured
my heart. Watching him age and become infirm was difficult.
During his last few years arthritis so crippled Luigi's front paws
that he stumbled along in a kind of army crawl when he walked.
Although he grew more and more sedate, spending the majority
of his days asleep, the old fire would kindle in his eyes whenever
he saw that Jane and I were about to take a walk. He still barked
at the mailman with the ferocity of a pit bull. As he grew weaker,
I found myself drawing uncomfortable parallels to my own experience of aging and pondering the kinds of theological questions one usually hears from small children. What does it feel
like to die? And after death, what then? Do dogs go to heaven?

I know that in the greater scheme of things the loss of a

family pet is trivial. In a world afflicted by poverty, war and cancer, it hardly seems worth grieving over. Yet grieve we did, weeping together as we waited in the veterinarian's office for the final arrangements to be made, and nodding through our tears as the staff expressed polite sympathy. The end when it came was as quick and painless as it was silent. The doctor administered two doses of anesthetic, one to put our dog to sleep, another to cause his tiny heart to stop beating. The vet made certain there was no pulse and expressed a final condolence for our family's loss. I stood crying and watched the light go out of Luigi's blind eyes.

I AM AFRAID OF DEATH

Those who have loved and lost a pet will understand how sad our quiet house seemed when we came home that day. There was no warning bark at the door. No click of paws greeted us as we stepped across the threshold into what was once our pup's sovereign domain. There was no frenzied wag of the tail. Only a profound and empty silence.

In the days that followed we appreciated the small words of comfort we received from friends who had shared a similar loss. Each friend acknowledged that they had experienced the same grief mixed with embarrassment. They too had tried to staunch the pain with a litany of cold comfort. "We shouldn't feel so bad," we told ourselves repeatedly. "We had many good years with him. And after all, he was only a dog." These words, although true to our reason and our theology, were remarkably inadequate under the circumstances.

Mark Twain once said, "Heaven goes by favor. If it went by merit, you would stay out and your dog would go in." In one of his poems John Updike observed that dogs possess all the virtues of man without his vices. But this is romanticism. My dog's behavior often reminded me that he was just an animal. He often did things that would make the most uncouth person shudder. Perhaps that is why the Bible, for the most part, portrays dogs as scavengers, ill-behaved and dangerous (Ps 22:16, 20; 59:6, 14; Jer 15:3). They return to their vomit, like the fool who repeats his folly (Prov 26:11; 2 Pet 2:22). They do not have a regard for what is sacred (Mt 7:6). This is figurative language for the most part. But it is hardly complimentary.

The theological questions that came to mind during those days of grief were as much about the nature of eternity as they were about dogs. I found it hard to imagine an eternity without my dog. It was even more difficult to picture an eternity in which I was not married to my wife, Jane. We have enjoyed so many things on earth together, it seemed only natural that we would explore the undiscovered country hand in hand. Yet in Matthew 22:30 Jesus says, "At the resurrection people will neither marry nor be given in marriage; they will be like the angels in heaven." Perhaps this was one of the reasons I found my dog's death so disturbing. Like a sudden chill at dusk, it heralded the coming of night and an unwelcome separation. Yet Jesus' example was meant to be positive rather than negative. It displays the power of God. In heaven our relationships are changed, not eliminated.

> I found it hard to imagine an eternity without my dog. It was even more difficult to picture an eternity in which I was not married to my wife.

In the lonely days that followed Luigi's death I found myself turning repeatedly to the words of Jesus in Luke 12:6: "Are not five sparrows sold for two pennies? Yet not one of them is forgotten by God." Jesus was talking about the sparrows that were used in temple sacrifices, not family pets. In Matthew 6:26 he speaks of the birds of the air, which do not sow or reap or store away in barns but are fed by God. In each case his point is the same. The God who cares for birds also cares for you. A God who remembers the sparrow when it falls will also remember you. Jesus' emphasis on God's remembering seemed especially appropriate, since memory was so much a part of our small grief.

Luigi was, after all, only a dog. Yet the lingering memory of his presence filled us with a grief disproportionate to the loss. Our little pup was gone. Yet something remained, a fleeting presence on the periphery of our experience. Somehow it made us more aware of his absence in death than we were of his presence in life. In some strange way Luigi's passing became a collecting point for all the losses of life: the death of our parents, the grief we felt over the years of exile from our family imposed by a life of ministry, the recollection of failed aspirations and the memory of broken promises. All these gathered at his grave. They were a reminder that this grief was only the small interest on a much greater accumulation of loss. Most of all, the death of our beloved dog reminded me of something I had known for some time but did not want to admit. I am afraid of death.

After his wife died, C. S. Lewis observed, "No one ever told me that grief felt so like fear. I am not afraid, but the sensation is like being afraid. The same fluttering in the stomach, the same restlessness, the yawning. I keep on swallowing."[1] Joan Didion described her experience of grief similarly in her memoir of the days that followed her husband's death. "Grief has no distance," Didion wrote. "Grief comes in waves, paroxysms, sudden apprehensions that weaken the knees and blind the eyes and obliterate the dailiness of life."[2] For me fear is grief's companion. The sorrow that I feel when someone I love has died is accompanied by a kind of panic. "What if it is not true?" a voice seems to whisper. "What if all this talk of hope and life after death is just whistling in the graveyard, a desperate effort to keep my mind off the inevitable?"

I know that I shouldn't fear death. The Scriptures tell me that Jesus shared my humanity so that he could "free those who all their lives were held in slavery by their fear of death" (Heb 2:15). I believe this is true. Yet I am still afraid. I know some Christians who are afraid of dying. But they fear the crossing, not the destination. I am anxious about both. I do not look forward to the dying. But I am also apprehensive about what comes next. I do not think I am alone in this. One reason for such fear is the alien nature of death.

THE MARGINALIZATION OF DEATH

We live in a culture that has insulated itself from death. As common as death is in human experience, we are rarely in its presence. "Poets, essayists, chroniclers, wags, and wise men write often about death but have rarely seen it," Sherwin B. Nuland notes. "Physicians and nurses, who see it often, rarely write about it. Most people see it once or twice in a lifetime, in situations where they are too entangled in its emotional significance to retain dependable memories."[3] On the few occasions when we do encounter death, we either see its effects from a distance or are removed from them altogether. "Nowadays, the style is to hide death from view," Nuland observes.[4]

There was a time when people died at home. They were embalmed and laid out at home too. Today most deaths in the United States take place in a hospital.[5] There the dying are isolated from the living, along with the disturbing changes wrought in the body by the onset of death. These are handled for us by paid professionals, who speedily remove the deceased from view and make up the bed. In a matter of minutes everything appears to have returned to normal. By all appearances the person might have risen from their bed of affliction and gone home. Or perhaps they merely relocated to another room. The transformation is so rapid, we could easily persuade ourselves that a dead body was never there at all. The next time we see the corpse (the word is harsh but it is the right word; this is no longer the living soul we once knew) it will be in the funeral home. There the body, from which the soul has now departed, will be laid in state in a coffin designed to look like a bed. With hands folded and dressed in their best clothes, the impression we get is not so much of one who has died but of someone who is merely asleep. This is the intent. The surroundings are designed to look like a living room, a legacy perhaps from the days when many funerals were conducted in the home. The overall effect is comforting. But it does add to the general sense of detachment.

Thomas G. Long is troubled by a further remove in the practice of the Christian funeral. In many funerals, "the frank acknowledgement of the pain of death and firm hope in the resurrection of the body" is being replaced by a popular liturgy of "vague, body-defying, death-defying, blather."[6] This kind of talk assures mourners that the deceased did not really die, while ignoring the blunt proof of the corpse. "Dead bodies, however, are definitely there, and they have become unfortunately an embarrassment to us, a vulgarity, so much so that we have arrived at a place unprecedented in history: conducting Christian funerals without the presence of the dead."[7] Long notes that our discomfort with the dead has led to the abandonment of traditional funeral rites in favor of new traditions that do not require the presence of the body and focus on life rather than death. These new funeral rites emphasize joy instead of grief, while celebrating the life of the deceased instead of acknowledging the reality of death. Long is bothered by this change. "I would like to suggest that these newer rituals, for all of their virtues of freedom, simplicity, and seeming festivity, are finally expressions of a corrupted understanding of the Christian view of death."[8] According to Long the function of the Christian funeral is to proclaim the gospel in word and action. The role of the church is to bear witness to the hope of Christ.

Media is a different matter. If the body is absent from many Christian funerals today, the landscape of popular media is teeming with corpses. Death is a common feature in many television dramas. Yet despite its prevalence, television death brings us no closer to the reality. Death usually plays only a marginal role in the story. In most programs death's presence is merely a backdrop for the dramatic interaction between the show's characters. Death is portrayed graphically but not necessarily realistically. The main characters, who are usually members of law enforcement or the medical profession, tend to be hardened toward the realities that accompany death. Some are amused (or bemused) by its gruesome effects. In some shows the dead are cut into pieces and subjected to a variety of tests in an effort to find clues that will lead to the killer. Although this is done in the name of justice, the corpse must be subjected to the worst kind of objectification in order to achieve this goal.

In other programs the effects of death are mitigated through supernatural means. These may be dark (as in the case of the increasing number of shows about vampires and zombies) or fantastic (as in the case of superheroes). This is especially a feature of many video games, where players can kill and be killed repeatedly without pain or consequences. Either way the message is essentially the same. Death is not the final enemy whose defeat can be accomplished only by the power of God. It is merely a temporary condition whose effects can be reversed. Hundreds (perhaps thousands) of studies have explored the effects of violence in various forms of media on behavior. We might also wonder how constant immersion in this romanticized media world has shaped our view of death. It seems as likely to produce a culture of denial as much as it does a culture of death. As a result we are as emotionally removed from the reality of death as we are physically removed from its effects. Like those who watch from a great distance, we learn to ignore death's sharp sting until it suddenly intrudes on us.

DEATH IS UNNATURAL

There is another reason that death seems so alien to us, even though it is common to all. According to the Scriptures, death entered human experience from the outside. Death came through sin (Gen 2:17). Death may be universal to human experience, but it is not "natural" in one important respect. Death was not part of humanity's original nature. Death intruded into human experience when Adam disobeyed God. Perhaps this is why death's arrival always seems to take us by surprise. We are often as stunned when someone dies after many years as we are at the untimely death of a child. Death's ubiquity is the empirical evidence that all humans share the guilt of Adam's sin. According to Romans 5:12, "Death came to all men, because all sinned."

This connection between sin and death helps explain one of the most disturbing aspects of Christ's death: its horrific brutality. Jesus did not merely die. He was hung on a cross after being violently mistreated. Sin certainly played a role in Jesus' arrest and execution. He was betrayed out of spite and executed as a matter of political expediency. But Jesus' death was more than an example of religious jealousy cooperating with an oppressive political system. God was also at work in these events in a mysterious way. The same Scripture that acknowledges that Jesus was put to death "with the help of wicked men" also asserts that this was done "by God's set purpose and foreknowledge" (Acts 2:23). Through the lens of sin, it looks like Jesus' life was taken from him. But through the lens of God's purpose and foreknowledge, we see a very different picture. Jesus laid down his life.

Christ's death is depicted in Scripture as an act of obedience rather than a tragedy. Death on the cross was more than the culminating event in Christ's incarnational experience; it was the very reason Jesus was made in human likeness. Jesus "became obedient to death—even death on a cross" (Phil 2:8). The analogy the Bible uses to explain this seeming contradiction comes from the Old Testament's system of sacrifice for sin. Jesus is the Lamb of God who takes away the sin of the world by means of his shed blood. He was "delivered over to death for our sins and was raised to life for our justification" (Rom 4:25). In a sense, those who put Jesus to death were like the knife wielded by the priest at the altar. God used their "sinful hands" to deliver a stroke that would eventually unravel both sin and death.

This relationship between sin, death and the cross also explains the Bible's ambivalence about death. Death has been defeated at the cross, yet we continue to suffer collateral damage from its reign. Death is an occasion for grief. It is the "last enemy" (1 Cor 15:26). Jesus wept at the tomb of dead Lazarus.

He was overcome with sorrow as he contemplated his own imminent death. We too feel ambivalent about death. The grief of believers may not be like those who have no hope, but it is still grief. There is more to death than a physical event. Death is also a spiritual condition that entered the human race the moment Adam disobeyed God's command. The Bible describes death as a coregent in the reign of sin (Rom 5:12-17). As such, death is not our friend but a dread enemy: "Yes, some deaths are more peaceful than others, some are less painful than others, some can even be taken to be blessings; but death itself is not holy."[9] Death is a curse. Indeed, it is *the* curse. Death has come to us as a result of Adam's sin and its ravages put a face on the deeper corruption that sin has wreaked on us. Death is the objective proof that all people everywhere need the forgiveness and grace that comes through Jesus Christ.

THE UNRAVELING OF DEATH

Jesus Christ dealt a decisive blow to death through the cross. Because of this, the apostle Paul felt genuinely torn as he contemplated the possibility of his own death. To continue to live in the body meant more opportunities for fruitful service and benefit for the church. But he concluded that as good as it was to remain alive, it was "better by far" for him to depart and be with Christ. Death as Paul describes it is merely an embarkation point (Phil 1:23). Dying is a transition from life to life. Nevertheless, we may look forward to being in Christ's presence and still feel anxious about death. Paul was eager to be with Christ, not for the experience of dying. No one looks forward to the dissolution of the body. Like the apostle, "we do not wish to be unclothed but to be clothed with our heavenly dwelling, so that what is mortal may be swallowed up by life" (2 Cor 5:4).

The greatest reason believers may still fear death is the difficulty we have grasping the nature of the life that follows. The blessed dead "rest from their labor" and "their deeds follow them" (Rev 14:13). But what is the precise nature of this rest? The few pictures we can find in Scripture describe a peculiar landscape, one not entirely different from our own world yet strange enough to seem alien. The work of heaven seems equally peculiar: a cacophony of mass prayer in multiple languages mixed with bowing and the casting off of crowns. None of this sounds especially interesting. At least not interesting enough to sustain our attention for an eternity. Perhaps if we examined the picture from a different angle, thinking of it more as a visual essay than a photograph, we would see things differently.

The apostle John gives us one of Scripture's most detailed depictions of heaven in the book of Revelation. It begins on earth with a vision of the risen Christ that is so strange and formidable that John "fell at his feet as though dead" (Rev 1:17). Things are not much different when he is invited to observe the worship of heaven. There John sees God's throne and before it a lamb. But this is not the lamb that we see so often depicted in church windows. This lamb is not fluffy and cute like my little dog. It is a lamb with seven horns, seven eyes and a perpetual wound (Rev 5:6). There are others near the throne as well. Countless angels are present, including four "living creatures" covered with eyes in front and back. Each of these four angelic beings has its own distinctive appearance. One is in the form of a lion, one is an ox, one a man and one a flying eagle (Rev 4:6-7). People are before the throne too. Twenty-four elders sit on thrones wearing white robes and golden crowns. They worship by prostrating themselves in front of the lamb and laying their crowns before his throne (Rev 4:4, 10). The angelic creatures and the elders cry out in hymns of praise. There is a vast multitude drawn from every nation, tribe, people and language. They stand before the lamb in white robes and holding palm branches. When these saints cry out in unison, all the angels of heaven fall on their faces to worship the lamb (Rev 7:11).

John seems to be doing something more here than painting a picture. There is a metaphoric quality to what he describes. But he is also pointing to events that have significance in the real world and in real time. In the book of Revelation John speaks of things that have already happened in the past and points forward to things yet to come. These are more than word pictures. They are a revelation of "what must soon take place" (Rev 1:1). There are ancient promises yet to be fulfilled. There is a kingdom to confer, one prepared since the foundation of the world. There are thrones and crowns that must be bestowed before the work of judging men and angels begins. There is a rest that remains and a world that is yet to come.

John describes this world, if ever so briefly, in his revelation. But it does not come until the final two chapters, where its features are sketched in broad outline. John's portrait is so spare that believers have used their imagination to fill in the gaps ever since. The result of these efforts, not surprisingly, looks much like the world in which we already live. How could it not be so? Ours is the only world we have experienced. When we try to imagine what the future world will be like, we can use only the frame of reference we already have. John's picture of the new heavens and the new earth also speaks in terms we already know. There is a city there and a river. There are trees (or at least one tree) and people. There may even be animals. Perhaps I will see my little pup again after all. Though I cannot help noting that John assigns dogs a place outside the city gates, with "those who practice magic arts, the sexually immoral, the murderers, the idolaters and everyone who loves and practices falsehood" (Rev 22:15). The location makes me suspect that he is speaking figuratively and not of real dogs at all.

By carefully attending to the Bible's peculiar vision, I get a glimpse of what final rest will be like. It shows me that there will be some continuity between this world and the next. There will also be significant differences. The new world will be a realm of light, without need for any lamp or sun. It will be a world without tears. In the world to come there will be no more death, mourning, crying or pain. It will be a world where the old order of things has passed away along with the curse. This is a world without evil, one from which Satan and all who serve him have been banished. It is a world where the rupture between heaven and earth will finally be healed. God's dwelling will be with us. It is a world where his will is done on earth as it is in heaven.

Even so, the vision is not as clear as I might have liked. Perhaps I was hoping for some kind of travel guide, the sort of thing they publish for those who plan to visit Disney World and the Magic Kingdom. After all the Bible has to say about the world to come, I don't really know what attractions await

> God will not forget us either in the hour of our death. I confess that I hope the same is true of pups.

me there. I don't know how I will spend my days, at least not in detail. What's more, I find that despite these assurances, my fear sometimes persists. But faith is greater than fear. And God is greater than my faith. Are not five sparrows sold for two pennies? Yet not one of them is forgotten by God. God will not forget us either in the hour of our death. I confess that I hope the same is true of pups. But if not, it can only mean that the love we will experience in the world to come will transcend the greatest loves we have known in this world.

THE PURSUIT OF RADICAL REST

John's vision was not intended to answer all my questions about the life to come. His aim was to hold out hope to those who struggle in the here and now. John's vision of the future is a reminder not to give up in my pursuit of rest. There is a rest that remains that is unlike anything I have yet experienced. I have been given a foretaste of it now but the reality that is to come will make what I have experienced seem pale by comparison. John's vision also reorients me in my pursuit of rest. Rest is not something I acquire by skill or even a state of being I achieve. As John pictures it, rest is something brought to me by God himself. I do not ascend to rest; it descends to me. Rest is a destination. But I must be carried if I am to reach it.

It is not the pursuit of rest that makes it radical but its nature. This is God's rest offered to me as a gift through Christ. I see now that this has been my problem all along. I somehow came to believe that it all depended on me. I was persuaded that my value was linked to what I produced. But I am weary of living in the church's world of total work. I have been beaten down by my own ambition. There is more to the Christian life than working for the church. There is more to rest than simply managing my life well. I cannot attain rest by measured effort. It begins with God and comes to me as a gift of grace. Radical rest will come to me at last, as sudden and surprising as a lover who greets me from behind. At that moment I will come fully awake, alive to God and perfect in my worship of him. This is what I was made for. God made me for himself. And I will always be restless, until I rest in him.

QUESTIONS FOR REFLECTION

1. How should Christians view death? Should we look forward to it? Why or why not?

2. In 1 Corinthians 15:26 the apostle Paul calls death "the last enemy to be destroyed." In what sense can it be said that death is still our "enemy"?

3. Media portrayals of death are both graphic and unrealistic. What does this communicate about death to the audience? How does it affect the way we view death?

4. Thomas Long criticizes the practice of some churches that conduct funerals without the presence of the dead. Do you think the presence of the dead is important to the funeral? Why or why not? What are the implications of removing the body from sight? Are there any advantages of keeping the dead in view?

5. How might John's description of final rest help us cope with the fear of death? What does it teach us about the nature of "final rest"?

6. What would you say to someone who told you they were afraid of death?

ACKNOWLEDGMENTS

Eugene Peterson's observation about pastoral ministry also holds true when it comes to the writing of books. It is not especially glamorous work. The writing of a book consists mostly of "modest, daily, assigned work." It is gratifying but it is also laborious. I need to express my thanks to many who make this work possible for me. I am especially grateful to editorial director Cindy Bunch and editor Helen Lee at InterVarsity Press. Cindy's enthusiastic response to my proposal came at a time when I was wondering whether I should continue to pursue my vocation as a writer. I took her interest to be a token from God that I might still have something to say and that there might be some who would want to read what I wrote. Associate editor Helen Lee's wise and gentle advice made this a much better book than it would otherwise have been. Her kind encouragement brought me in off the ledge at several crucial moments. Thanks go to Kristi Reimer for her excellent work as the copyeditor for this project. She deftly smoothed out the rough edges in my work while retaining my voice. I am grateful to her for making me sound better than I deserve.

Writing for InterVarsity feels a little like coming home for me. I was a very young Christian when I first became involved with their campus ministry at Wayne State University in Detroit. InterVarsity taught me how to study the Bible and provided the DNA for many of the ministry skills I continue to practice today. Campus staff worker John Natelborg (now retired) became a lifelong friend.

I also am thankful for the advocacy of my agent Mark Sweeney. His strong encouragement is always combined with good counsel. Mark Galli, editor-in-chief of *Christianity Today*, has done me a great honor by writing the foreword for this project. Mark's enthusiasm for my work has meant much to me over the years. His article "Whatever Happened to Grace?" in the October 2013 issue of *Christianity Today* was the shot over the bow that first got me thinking about this subject.

I am profoundly grateful for the loving support of my wife, Jane, who always reads every word I write. She is my chief fan and my best critic. Her praise means more to me than anyone else. Most of all I am grateful to God who spoke the first word and to Jesus Christ who is the Father's last Word. Thank you for the gift of language and the skill to use it. Thank you for the ministry of the indwelling Holy Spirit, who speaks to me through the words of Scripture. Grant us your rest both now and in the life to come.

QUESTIONS *for*
GROUP DISCUSSION

CHAPTER 1: RESTLESS FAITH
Read Matthew 11:28–12:14.

1. Name someone you consider to be a successful leader. What is it about that person that makes others want to follow him or her? How does this person differ from other leaders?

2. What do you think Jesus' listeners would have found most surprising about the invitation Jesus issues in Matthew 11:28-30? Do you think the image of the yoke would have seemed attractive or repulsive to them? Why?

3. What purpose did a yoke serve for the animal who wore it? What does the image suggest about Jesus' intent for those who follow him?

4. What surprising action did the disciples take in Matthew 12:1? Why was this unusual? How did the religious leaders react? What did they expect Jesus to do? What did he do instead?

5. How did Jesus justify the actions of his disciples? How did Jesus' reaction differ from the religious leaders'? How is his response an example of the easy yoke?

6. Where do you need to experience the easy yoke of Christ most today? What do you think is keeping you from experiencing the rest of Christ?

CHAPTER 2: THE GOD WHO RESTS

Read Genesis 1:1–2:3.

1. Do you think it's important to believe that God created the world? Why or why not? How does Genesis 1:1–2:3 portray God's relationship to the world in which we live? What does the biblical writer seem to be emphasizing in this account?

2. In what ways does the creator differ from creation in these verses? God's involvement with creation seems to follow a pattern that is reflected in the three phrases: "God said," "God called" and "God saw." What is the significance of each of these phrases?

3. Moses portrays God as the primary actor in this account. Creation owes its origin to God. Is there anything creation does for itself (see Gen 1:22, 24, 28)?

4. How does the creation of humanity compare with what has gone before? How is it similar? How does it differ? How does humanity itself differ from the rest of creation? How does the role of humanity differ from that of the other creatures God made?

5. Since God never grows weary, why do you think he rested on the seventh day? What does the rest of God say about creation? What does it say about humanity?

6. In John 5:17 Jesus defends himself against those who criticized him for healing on the Sabbath by saying, "My Father

is always at his work to this very day, and I, too, am working." What does this imply about the rest spoken of in Genesis 2:2?

7. How does it change your view of God to think of him as being "at rest" and "always at his work"? Does this have any implication for our own activity? How can we be "at work" for God while we are "at rest"?

CHAPTER 3: BEYOND THE DAY OF REST

Read Matthew 6:19-33.

1. Is it wrong for a Christian to have a savings account or a retirement account? Why or why not? What is the difference between financial stewardship and "storing up treasure"?

2. What is the difference between treasures "on earth" and "in heaven"? In view of Jesus' warning in verse 20, what kinds of things are being stored up? For what purpose? How do we go about "storing" treasures in heaven (see Mt 6:1-18)?

3. How does Jesus describe the connection between heart, eyes and body in verses 21 to 23? What, according to Jesus, do our treasures say about us?

4. In what way does "vision" shape our behavior? Is vision as Jesus describes it simply a matter of looking? Or does he have something else in mind?

5. In verse 24 Jesus warns of the danger of making money (literally "Mammon") our master. In verse 33 he points us to the kingdom. Is there a difference between serving a master and seeking the kingdom? Is there any similarity?

6. Are the concerns raised in verse 31 trivial? Is "worrying" about these things the same as "running after" them? What reasons does Jesus give for not responding this way?

7. How do we "seek first his kingdom and his righteousness"? Is this a promise of prosperity (see verse 34)? What is promised?

CHAPTER 4: FALSE REST

Read Numbers 14:1-24.

1. Verses 1 to 4 describe Israel's reaction to the majority report issued by those who were sent on the first reconnaissance mission into Canaan. How strong was their response? Why did they react this way? Do you think their response was reasonable or unreasonable? Why?

2. What do Moses and Aaron do when they hear the people's complaint? Why do you think they react this way (see Num 16:4, 22, 45; 20:6)? How do Joshua and Caleb react? How does God respond?

3. What do Joshua and Caleb see that the rest of the people do not? How do they evaluate the people's behavior? How does God evaluate Israel's behavior?

4. What does God propose to do in verse 12? Why does Moses think this is the wrong course of action? How does Moses' "disagreement" with God differ from Israel's? Why didn't God get angry with Moses for objecting to his plan?

5. What judgment does God pronounce on Israel instead? Israel reacts to this with mourning and a new determination to enter the land God has promised to them. Why isn't this repentance? Why might it be said that God gave those who rebelled exactly what they asked for?

6. If we think of sloth as evading responsibility and ignoring opportunity, when do you struggle most with sloth? How

do you feel when you succumb to sloth? How might changing your perspective of God help you resist this temptation?

CHAPTER 5: REST AND AMBITION

Read Mark 10:34-45.

1. Why does the success of others sometimes make us feel anxious? Is it because we are happier when they fail? In his book *Status Anxiety* author Alain de Botton observes that we are most inclined to envy those who are most like us. Why is this?

2. What request do James and John make of Jesus? What is the significance of being seated on Jesus' right and left hand? What seems to have prompted this request (see Mk 10:32-34)? How did Jesus respond?

3. What question does Jesus ask James and John in response to their request? How do they answer? Why do you think Jesus did not reprove them for making such a request?

4. How did the other disciples react to James and John? What do you think bothered them most? How do you think you would have reacted in this situation? Why?

5. How does Jesus' definition of greatness differ from that of the Gentiles? Why do you think Jesus singles out Gentile rulers? What do leadership and servanthood have in common with each other? What does it mean to be "slave of all"?

6. In what areas of your life do you need to exemplify the kind of servanthood that Jesus describes in these verses? What would that look like?

CHAPTER 6: WORSHIP AS REST

Read 1 Corinthians 14:23-40.

1. What do you like most about the worship of your church? What do you like least? Do the things you dislike make it difficult for you to worship? Why or why not?

2. These verses give a description of some of the practices in Corinthian worship. Does Paul affirm these practices or criticize them? What is his main concern? Do you think the guidelines he describes in these verses still apply to congregational worship? Why or why not?

3. Although some Christians disagree about whether the specific gifts mentioned in these verses should be considered normative today, they all seem to have something in common. What is it? Does this say anything about where the focal point of our worship should be?

4. Do you think Paul would endorse "seeker-sensitive" worship? What kind of experience does he expect the seeker to have according to verses 24 and 25? What kind of experience do you think he expects the believer to have?

5. What primary guideline does Paul provide for evaluating worship practices in verse 26? How do we determine whether this guideline is being met by our own practices?

6. According to this passage, what happens when we encounter God's Word? Does this happen only through the sermon (see 1 Cor 11:23-26)? What role should music play in this?

7. If you were to design the church's worship service, what would it look like? What elements would you include? What order would you place them in?

CHAPTER 7: REST AND THE DIGITAL AGE

Read Acts 2:42-47.

1. Take a few minutes to look around the room. How many items of technology can you identify? Where are you most affected by digital technology? On the whole, would you describe digital culture as a blessing or a curse? Why?

2. Acts 2:42-47 gives a brief description of community life in the early church. Do you think digital culture would have enhanced or detracted from this experience? What kinds of technology shaped the experience of the early church?

3. How does digital community differ from the kind of experiences described in these verses? What possibilities for community does digital culture create? What is digital community unable to do that these believers were able to do?

4. In verse 44 Luke says that these believers "were together and had everything in common." But the common life of the early church also brought problems (see Acts 5:1-5; 6:1). In what ways can digital culture tempt us to be too idealistic in our expectations of Christian community? How is embodied life a good remedy for this?

5. Dietrich Bonhoeffer described Christian community as "life together." But in what sense is it also a "life apart"? How has digital culture eroded your ability to do "life apart"? Is this primarily a technological problem or something else? What steps should you take to address this?

6. Neil Postman has warned about the danger of unintended consequences when it comes to technology. How can your church be more reflective about the spiritual implications of the technology we use? Are there any areas of particular concern? Who should you talk to about them?

CHAPTER 8: REST AND THE FUTURE

Read 2 Samuel 7:1-29.

1. Do you tend to have a positive or negative view of the future? Why do you think this is? Where does this show up in your life? How does this compare to other Christians you know?

2. What prompted David to decide that he should "build a house" for God? Do you think he was being presumptuous in this? Why or why not? How did the prophet respond to David's proposal? How did God respond? How would you explain the difference?

3. What reasons did God give for changing David's plans? What promises did God make? Who is involved in these promises besides David? How far into the future did God's plans reach? Why might it be said that we were also included in these plans?

4. How did rest figure into David's plan for God's house? How did rest figure into God's plan for David? What do you think God was trying to teach David by this?

5. According to verse 21, why did God alter David's plans? What evidence can you find in David's prayer that he understood he was part of a larger plan? Who else was included in God's plans for David?

6. What is it about the future that most concerns you today? Does it help to think that God's plans for you are part of a much larger plan? Spend some time expressing your concerns about the future to God.

CHAPTER 9: FINAL REST

Read Revelation 21:1–22:5.

1. John's description has been the focus of considerable specu-

lation. As you read these verses, do you think it is better to approach them like a photograph or a painting? How does each perspective change the way you view John's depiction?

2. What are the main features of the new world that John describes? Does it have anything in common with the old creation? How do they differ?

3. What metaphor does John use to describe the Holy City? What do you think he is trying to tell us about it with this image? What is its point of origin? How is it described? What is its most significant feature? Why do you think the city is also called "the bride" in verse 9?

4. Do sinners disappear from view in John's picture? Where are they? Why do you think the fiery lake of burning sulfur is included in this description? According to Revelation 22:15 the dogs, those who practice magic arts, the sexually immoral, murderers, the idolaters and everyone who loves and practices falsehood are situated "outside" the city. What does this imply about them? What does it say about their fate?

5. According to Revelation 22:6, how should we regard the picture John has provided for us of the world to come? Is it possible to accept these words as "trustworthy and true" and still be afraid of death? What would you say to someone who was in such a condition?

6. Wanting to die is not the same thing as being prepared to die. What is the difference? Are you prepared to die?

NOTES

INTRODUCTION

[1]Josef Pieper, *Only the Lover Sings: Art and Contemplation* (San Francisco: Ignatius Press, 1990), 19.

CHAPTER 1: RESTLESS FAITH

[1]National Sleep Foundation, "2015 Sleep in America Poll: Sleep and Pain Summary of Findings" (Arlington, VA: 2015), 12.

[2]Neil Postman, *Technopoly* (New York: Vintage, 1993), 13.

[3]Mark Galli, "Whatever Happened to Grace?," *Christianity Today*, October 2013, 24.

[4]Josef Pieper, *Leisure: The Basis of Culture* (San Francisco: Ignatius, 2009), 25.

[5]Ibid., 67-69.

[6]Ibid., 33.

[7]Ibid., 35-36.

[8]Wendell Berry, *The Art of the Commonplace: The Agrarian Essays of Wendell Berry* (Berkley: Counterpoint, 2002), 19.

[9]Ibid.

[10]Ibid.

[11]St. Augustine, *The Confessions of St. Augustine*, ed. Rosalie De Rosset (Chicago: Moody Publishers, 2007), 19.

CHAPTER 2: THE GOD WHO RESTS

[1]F. F. Bruce, *The Epistle to the Hebrews* (Grand Rapids: Eerdmans, 1964), 74.

[2]John Stott, *God's New Society: The Message of Ephesians* (Downers Grove, IL: InterVarsity Press, 1979), 81.

[3]Josef Pieper, *Only the Lover Sings: Art and Contemplation* (San Francisco: Ignatius, 1990), 25.

CHAPTER 3: BEYOND THE DAY OF REST

[1] Susannah Heschel in the introduction to Abraham Joshua Heschel's *The Sabbath* (New York: Farrar, Straus and Giroux, 1951), vii.

[2] Stephen Miller, *The Peculiar Life of Sundays* (Cambridge: Harvard, 2008), 21.

[3] Richard J. Bauckham, "Sabbath and Sunday in the Post-Apostolic Church," in *From Sabbath Day to Lord's Day*, ed. D. A. Carson (Eugene, OR: Wipf and Stock, 1982), 255.

[4] A. T. Lincoln observes that the move to Sunday observance was probably not a Pauline innovation. This would have been met with disapproval by his opponents and some record of the dispute would appear in the New Testament. Instead, it seems more likely that Palestinian Jewish Christians already gathered on the first day of the week even before the gospel spread to the Gentiles. According to Lincoln, "The majority of Jewish Christians in Palestine and many in the diaspora may well have kept the Sabbath and also met with their fellow believers in Christ for worship at some time on the following day." See "From Sabbath to Lord's Day: A Biblical and Theological Perspective," in *From Sabbath Day to Lord's Day*, 384.

[5] Richard H. Lowery, *Sabbath and Jubilee* (St. Louis: Chalice, 2000), 3.

[6] Dallas Willard, *The Spirit of the Disciplines* (San Francisco: HarperCollins, 1991), 153.

[7] Geerhardus Vos, *Biblical Theology* (Grand Rapids: Eerdmans, 1948), 141.

[8] Helmut Thielicke, *The Prayer That Spans the World: Sermons on the Lord's Prayer* (Cambridge, UK: James Clarke & Co., 1978), 83.

CHAPTER 4: FALSE REST

[1] Dorothy Sayers, *Letters to a Diminished Church* (Nashville: Thomas Nelson, 2004), 97.

[2] Ibid.

[3] Ibid., 97-98.

[4] Anthony Bloom, *Beginning to Pray* (New York: Paulist, 1970), 81.

[5] Ibid., 85.

[6] Ibid., 90.

[7] Wendell Berry, *The Art of the Commonplace: The Agrarian Essays of Wendell Berry* (Berkeley: Counterpoint, 2009), 186.

[8] Ibid.

[9] Ibid., 187.

[10]Ibid.

[11]Eugene Peterson, *Under the Unpredictable Plant: An Exploration in Vocational Holiness* (Grand Rapids: Eerdmans, 1992), 16-17.

CHAPTER 5: REST AND AMBITION

[1]Neil Strauss, "God at the Grammys: The Chosen Ones," *The Wall Street Journal*, February 12, 2011.

[2]Alain de Botton, *Status Anxiety* (New York: Pantheon, 2004), 87.

[3]Richard Lischer, *Open Secrets: A Spiritual Journey Through a Country Church* (New York: Doubleday, 2001), 8.

[4]Ibid., 8-9.

[5]Jen Pollock Michel, *Teach Us to Want: Longing, Ambition and the Life of Faith* (Downers Grove, IL: InterVarsity Press, 2014), 29.

[6]Wendell Berry, *The Art of the Commonplace: The Agrarian Essays of Wendell Berry* (Berkeley: Counterpoint, 2002), 211.

[7]William Dyrness, *How Does America Hear the Gospel?* (Grand Rapids: Eerdmans, 1989), 98.

[8]Ibid.

[9]Skye Jethani, *The Divine Commodity* (Grand Rapids: Eerdmans, 2009), 55.

[10]Bob Smietana, "Who Owns the Sermons?," *Christianity Today*, January/February 2014, 48-51.

[11]Jean Kilbourne, "Jesus Is a Brand of Jeans," *New Internationalist*, September 2006, 10-12.

[12]Ibid.

CHAPTER 6: WORSHIP AS REST

[1]Josef Pieper, *Only the Lover Sings: Art and Contemplation* (San Francisco: Ignatius, 1990), 19.

[2]Josef Pieper, *Leisure: The Basis for Culture* (San Francisco: Ignatius, 1963), 46.

[3]Pieper, *Only the Lover Sings*, 23.

[4]James K. A. Smith, *Desiring the Kingdom: Worship, Worldview, and Cultural Formation* (Grand Rapids: Baker, 2009), 137.

[5]Ibid., 150-51.

[6]Pieper, *Only the Lover Sings*, 23.

[7]Donald G. Bloesch, *The Church: Sacraments, Worship, Ministry, Mission* (Downers Grove, IL: InterVarsity Press, 2002), 121.

[8]Thomas G. Long, *Preaching from Memory to Hope* (Louisville: Westminster John Knox, 2009), 35.

[9]Rudolf Otto, *The Idea of the Holy* (Oxford, UK: Oxford University Press, 1923), 12-24.

[10]Ibid., 26.

[11]Eugene Peterson, *Reversed Thunder: The Revelation of John and the Praying Imagination* (New York: Harper and Row, 1988), 59.

[12]Otto, *Idea of the Holy*, 41.

[13]Geerhardus Vos, *Biblical Theology* (Grand Rapids: Eerdmans, 1948), 70.

[14]Eugene Peterson, *Leap Over a Wall: Earthy Spirituality for Everyday Christians* (San Francisco: HarperSanFrancisco, 1997), 60-61.

[15]Donald W. McCullough, *The Trivialization of God: The Dangerous Illusion of a Manageable Deity* (Colorado Springs: NavPress, 1995), 110.

[16]Cited by Kenneth L. Woodward in "Dead End for the Mainline?," *Newsweek*, August 9, 1993, 46-48.

[17]Stanley Hauerwas, *Vision and Virtue: Essays in Christian Ethical Reflection* (Notre Dame, IN: University of Notre Dame Press, 1981), 45-46.

[18]Eugene Peterson, *Reversed Thunder*, 71.

CHAPTER 7: REST AND THE DIGITAL AGE

[1]Jennifer Senior, *All Joy and No Fun: The Paradox of Modern Parenthood* (New York: HarperCollins, 2014), 219.

[2]Quoted by Brigid Schulte in *Overwhelmed: Work, Love, and Play When No One Has Time* (New York: Farrar, Straus, & Giroux, 2014), 26.

[3]Dallas Willard, *The Spirit of the Disciplines: Understanding How God Changes Lives* (San Francisco: HarperSanFrancisco, 1988), 160.

[4]Ibid., 161.

[5]Josef Pieper, *Leisure: The Basis of Culture* (San Francisco: Ignatius Press, 1952), 46.

CHAPTER 8: REST AND THE FUTURE

[1]Charles Bridges, *Ecclesiastes* (Carlisle, PA: Banner of Truth, 1981), 286.

[2]Stanley Hauerwas, *A Cross-Shattered Church: Reclaiming the Theological Heart of Preaching* (Grand Rapids: Brazos, 2009), 90.

[3]C. S. Lewis, "The Efficacy of Prayer," in *The World's Last Night and Other Essays* (San Diego: Harcourt Brace Jovanovich, 1960), 10.

[4]Ibid., 11.

[5]David Bentley Hart, *The Doors of the Sea: Where Was God in the Tsunami?* (Grand Rapids: Eerdmans, 2005), 50.

[6]Robert Alter, *The David Story* (New York: W. W. Norton, 1999), 232.

[7]C. S. Lewis, *The Great Divorce* (New York: MacMillan, 1946), 68.

[8]Gilbert Meilaender, "Thinking About Aging," *First Things*, April 2011, 37-43.

[9]Stanley Hauerwas and Laura Yordy, "Captured in Time: Friendship and Aging," in *Growing Old in Christ*, ed. Stanley Hauerwas, Carole Bailey Stoneking, Keith G. Meador and David Cloutier (Grand Rapids: Eerdmans, 2003), 170.

[10]Maxine Hancock, "Aging as a Stage of the Heroic Pilgrimage of Faith: Some Literary and Theological Lenses for 'Re-Visioning' Age," *Crux* 47, no. 1 (2011): 2-14.

CHAPTER 9: FINAL REST

[1]C. S. Lewis, *A Grief Observed* (Toronto: Bantam, 1961), 1.

[2]Joan Didion, *The Year of Magical Thinking* (New York: Vintage, 2005), 27.

[3]Sherwin B. Nuland, *How We Die: Reflections on Life's Final Chapter* (New York: Alfred A. Knopf, 1993), 8.

[4]Ibid., 254.

[5]Ibid., 255.

[6]Thomas G. Long, *Accompany Them with Singing: The Christian Funeral* (Louisville: Westminster John Knox, 2009), 30.

[7]Ibid., 31.

[8]Ibid., 59.

[9]Ibid., 27.